HOPE
— FOR —
TOMORROW

GOD IS A FAITHFUL PROMISE KEEPER.
HE WILL BRING YOU OUT OF EVERY STORM.

KORNAH FLOWERS

Copyright © 2018 Kornah Flowers
All rights reserved
First Edition

PAGE PUBLISHING, INC.
New York, NY

First originally published by Page Publishing, Inc. 2018

ISBN 978-1-64350-400-1 (Paperback)
ISBN 978-1-64350-401-8 (Digital)

Printed in the United States of America

To my parents,
Rev. Rudolph and Nancy Williams Flowers (deceased).

Introduction

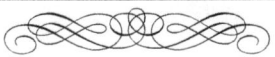

Mama's Best

Make something great and beautiful of your leftovers. Life is full of issues. Most times, you will find yourself in a situation or coming out of a situation or about to get in a situation. That is just the circle of life that leads to growth and maturity if perceived and acted upon with faith. Situation reveals the power of God in a way you have not known before, when you choose to stretch your faith, and believe God for the impossible to become possible.

Perception plays a major role in creating solutions. How you view people and situations is how you are going to deal with them.

Short story: In my childhood days, my precious mother, Nancy Williams Flowers, cooked a meal four days a week and froze the leftovers from each day. On Saturdays, she defrosted all the leftovers and made a delicious meal called Mama's best, which she joyfully served us. It tasted so good. It tasted like the best thing we had all week. Mama put her best into cooking and turned her leftovers one great delicious meal.

Sometimes your leftovers in life are frustrations, unfair treatments, loss of love ones, bad relationships, loss of property, etc.

Sometimes, it is not what happened to us in life that changes our lives for the better or worse but what we make of what happened.

You owe it to yourself and those who look up to you to make something great and beautiful of your life's leftovers. Start now. Start where you are with what you have. Everything big starts small.

Chapter 1

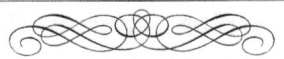

There's A Better Tomorrow for You, Despite the Odds

You may have started wrong, but you can end right. There is a better tomorrow for you despite the odds of your past or the struggles of your present. For every lock, there is a key. To every question, there is an answer. To every problem, there is a solution. When we discover the hidden solutions, then we recover from our current problems. It is time to discover so you can recover and move forward.

You may have started with nothing, but you can end up with everything you have ever dreamed of. You may have come from a despised and humble background, but you can end up at the very top being celebrated and highly recognized. You may have started as a captive that has been held in prison mentally, emotionally, spiritually, morally, financially, domestically, racially, academically, medically, socially and even physically; however, you can end up free. The choice is yours, only *believe* and never give up.

Only believe. Your condition is never your conclusion in Life, but an aspiration for transformation to a better destination. Anything is possible, and everything is subject to change no matter how long it has been in place. Your tomorrow is more beautiful than your today; therefore, imagine your present as your past and your future as your present. You cannot rewrite your past, but you can create a very beautiful future. Your past is like spilled water in the cultivated soil of life. Just as you cannot pick up the spilled water, so you can't change your past. Yesterday is gone. Today is moving fast to an end. Tomorrow is coming quicker than you have realized. What you don't have Today, you will have surplus tomorrow if you do things different. Start first by thinking *beautiful thoughts* about your future despite the odds of your past and the struggles of your present.

We become what we consistently think, believe, say, and do. Don't let your history dictate your destiny. Great men and women do not live and strive because of their history. They do because they believe in an ongoing multiplying greater destiny.

Your beautiful destiny is saying your name aloud. Will you answer the call, rise up, and begin to accomplish the responsibilities required to fulfill your destiny? In most cases, if you will reach the peak of your destiny, you must practice going beyond the normal requirements. When you consistently set higher standards for yourself, you will always succeed with a wild margin. Self-discipline is the engine behind great accomplishment.

You must begin to prayerfully develop the spirit of belief, despite the reality of the odds and the spirit of endurance and sacrifice despite your physical weakness. You must develop the spirit of persistence and relentless increasing actions despite the reality of unseen spiritual oppositions, physical barriers, obstacles, sudden situations, and circumstances. Remember, patience and persistence always get the job done. Resistance always gives way to persistence and situations are always overcome by determination.

Now is the time for you to rise up and be all that God created you to be. Only you can close the door on your beautiful future by embracing old thoughts, ignoring current opportunities, and being unprepared for what lies ahead. When you dwell on your past, the present will pass you by, and the future will erase the very mark of your existence.

A new and beautiful future starts with a new and beautiful mind-set. Don't let your mind-set, emotions, surroundings, and actions become roadblocks to your future; instead, let them become assets and gateways to your beautiful unending destinies.

It's never about where you are but who you are. For example: In America, a one-hundred-dollars bill does not change its value whether it's found on the ground, at a dumpster or in a building on a marble polished floor. It is still valued as one hundred dollars despite how dirty it might look. Whether you are locked up in prison, sick in the hospital, working a terrible job, or just surrounded by people with bad character, let the good in you come out.

Every vehicle is priced based upon its manufacturer and built-in functions. The purpose of each vehicle or product is to expose the manufacturer. That's why the vehicle carries the name of the manufacturer. A Mercedes could be muddy and dirty because of the road and weather conditions, but it does not lose its value. It is still an expensive vehicle because of its manufacturer. In the same way, you are a good person with a greater destiny awaiting you based upon your manufacturer. You were built to make it, overcome obstacles, and succeed. The dirt or flaws you have accumulated because of the weather and road conditions of life do not define you or change your value. You were made in the image and likeness of God.

> So God created man in His own image, in the image of God created He him; male and female created He them. (Genesis 1:27 KJV)

> And God saw everything that he had made, and behold, it was very good. And the evening and the morning were the sixth day. (Genesis 1:31 KJV)

It is so wrong to allow your history to determine your destiny or to let your past control your future. You may have started wrong, but you can end right. What matters most is not how you start but always how you finish. Exits are more important than entries, so we must learn to finish well on time and always try to leave on a great note. You can start school, but if you don't finish school and graduate, you will never earn the diploma, degree, position, and salary you deserved. You may have started wrong, but you don't have to end wrong. You have an opportunity to end right and victorious. No individual or team is awarded a trophy or championship for starting the game or race right, only for *ending right*.

Life is the greatest privilege anyone can have. Waking up every morning with a sound mind and energy is the greatest blessing many take for granted. You have *life*, a mind, and energy. This means you have the choice to *start new* and *end right*. *You* can make that decision *now*. *Now* is the only time you really have.

As it is often said, "A man does not drown when he falls into the river. He drowns when he remains there." *Falling down is not failure*. Failure is refusing to get back up when you fall and do things different consistently.

Failure is doing the same thing the same way and expecting a different result. Everybody falls when he or she is learning to walk as a baby. Even as adults, we sometimes accidently trip and fall. Everyone has a situational fall every now and then. Everyone falls occasionally, but wise and great people rise up quickly and do things differently.

Let Go of Your Past

Dwelling on your past hinders you from reaching the greatness of your future. Dwelling on your past causes you to live in the past, prevents you from making the most of your present, and blinds you from seeing the beauty of your future.

Let the past go, enjoy the present, and passionately reach for your future. I would like to refer to some references from the most advanced spiritual and practical book of all mankind—the Bible.

> Forget the former things; do not dwell on the past. See, I am doing a new thing! Now it springs up; do you not perceive it? I am making a way in the wilderness and streams in the wasteland. (Isaiah 43:18–19 NIV)

Don't dwell on what's wrong; instead, celebrate what's right. God will give you the grace to miraculously strengthen the weak areas in your life. Dwelling on your past successes or failures has the potential to place a stopper on your accomplishment of greater things tomorrow. Sometimes, convenience can rob us of achieving a greater destiny.

It causes you to have a sense that you have arrived. That is to say, you know it all and you have done it all. The great Apostle Paul, scholar and writer of two-thirds of the Bible, by the inspiration of the Holy Spirit said the following:

> Not that I have already obtained all this, or have already arrived at my goal, but I press on to take hold of that for which Christ took hold of me. Brothers and sisters, I do not consider myself yet to have taken hold of it. But one thing I do: Forgetting what is behind and straining toward what is ahead, I press toward the goal to win the prize for which God has called me heavenward in Christ Jesus. (Philippians 3:12–14)

Arrival leads to departure. When you arrive, you depart. In the secular world, when you serve your full term required by your job, you must retire. There must always be something greater, big or small, to work toward as long as you have life. God made work as part of the sustainer of human life.

When you stop learning, you stop knowing. When you stop knowing, you stop improving, so you become irrelevant to your society. You become a liability instead of an asset. Anything that stops working is gotten rid of. For example, if your watch stops working, you get rid of it. In order to keep working, you must stay current and keep advancing in every aspect of your life and ministry.

> My people are destroyed from the lack of knowledge. (Hosea 4:6)

When the Apostle Paul arrived at the finished line of his divine assignment, this is what he said which confirms that arrival and full completion leads to departure from the scene of relevance.

> And the time of my departure is near. I have fought a good fight, I have finished the race, I have kept the faith. Now there is store for me the crown of righteousness. (2 Timothy 4:6–8)

Stop talking about your bad past experiences and start talking about your beautiful, wonderful future just ahead of you.

- Self-discipline is the engine behind great accomplishment.

- Your condition is never your conclusion in life but an aspiration for transformation to a better destination.

- Patience and persistence always get the job done.

- Resistance always gives way to persistence and situations are always overcome by determination.

- Great men and women do not live and strive because of their history. They do because they believe in an ongoing multiplying greater destiny.

- When you dwell on your past, the present will pass you by, and the future will erase the very mark of your existence.

- Don't let the things you are ashamed of cause you to miss out on the things you will be proud of. Look to your future not your past.

Chapter 2

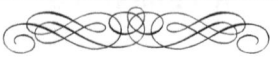

Forgiveness Settles All Matters, Not Revenge

Forgiveness settles all matters, not revenge. Forgiveness is God's tool to solve and end problems; whereas, unforgiveness is the devil's tool to continue and increase the problem. When you don't forgive, you are working for the devil. When you forgive, you are working for God. Who are you working for right now? Who you work for is who you get paid by.

> You've got to be different to make a difference.

The devil pays robbery, death, and destruction in any and all types and forms. God pays abundant life, eternal life, deliverance, healing, wholeness, peace, love, joy, favor, promotion, unlimited blessings in all types and forms. Right now, you can resign immediately from working for the devil by forgiving your offenders. Your name will automatically be removed of the payroll of robbery, death, and destruction.

> The thief cometh not, but for to steal, and to kill, and to destroy; I am come that they might have life and that they have it more abundantly. (John 10:10)

Bitterness is a major hindrance to a happy and successful life. Be quick to forgive. Hurt embraced, always stop the flow of love to the one who hurt you.

Why Forgive Your Offenders?

   A. Everyone needs forgiveness, including you. "For all have sinned and come short of the glory of God" (Romans 3:23). There is no big sin or small sin. None is good by himself. We become the righteousness of God only in Christ Jesus.
   B. What you give is what you get. What you send out will multiply and come back to you. What you sow is what you reap. "Give and it shall be given unto you good measured, pressed down, and shaken together, and running over, shall men give into your bosom. For with the same measure that ye mete withal it shall be measured to you again" (Luke 6:38). No matter how wrong a person is, if you choose not to forgive them, you also will not be forgiven of your faults, mistakes, or sins. Whoever sows unforgiveness reaps unforgiveness.

It is impossible to sow apple seeds and reap oranges at harvest time. In the same way, it is impossible to sow unforgiveness, bitterness, or hate and expect to reap forgiveness and love in the return. Remember, everything you think, say, and do is a seed you are sowing. Seeds have the potential to grow, multiply, and reproduce an ongoing greater harvest. It's time to repent and begin to sow goods seeds so that you can reap a better harvest. The truth is, your forgiveness from God depends on your forgiveness to others.

Matthew 6:12 says, "And forgive us our debts, as we forgive our debtors."

When you choose not forgive others, every time you talk about your bad experience with them, it makes you more angry.

Even the mention of their name in your presence makes you upset. It's time to let the past go.

As a believer, dwelling on your past is walking in disobedience to God's Word. "Therefore, if any man be in Christ, he is a new creature: old things are passed away; behold all things become new" (2 Corinthians 5:17). Decide whose view you will pursue, believe, and maintain about yourself—the view about your past experiences or the view in God's Word about your glorious future. Take your pick. "Do not be overcome by evil but overcome evil with good" (Romans 12:21). God's love is the key that sets people free because it is unconditional.

Unforgiveness is a trap that keeps you stuck in an invisible offensive environment. An offense is something that bothers you and makes you upset. Why hold on to something that is bothering you? Your freedom is in your own hands. Anything offensive stinks. Therefore, let go of that stinking thing. Why carry, inhale and exhale the odor of a stinking load that makes you upset every time you think or talk about it? You are smelling that offensive odor that comes from the load of bitterness you chose to carry day and night. You don't have to carry the load of bitterness any longer. Drop it at the cross of Jesus right now. He died for your peace and freedom. Place it all in God's hands so that your process of healing and elevation can begin. God's hands have healing for you and justice for your enemies if they do not repent. Take all your issues to the LORD in prayer.

Physical medicine can only heal the body sometimes, but prayers can heal the spirit, soul, and body all the times.

> Do not take revenge, my dear friends, but leave room for God's wrath, for it is written: "It is mine to avenge; I will repay," says the Lord. (Romans 12:19)

The measure of forgiveness you give to your offenders is the same measure of forgiveness you will receive from God. Read Matthew 18:21–35 for more understanding. "Shouldn't you have mercy on your fellow servant just as I had on you?" (Matthew 18:33).

- Forgiveness settles all matters, not revenge.

- Forgiveness is God's tool to solve and end problems; whereas, unforgiveness is the devil's tool to continue and increase the problem.

- When you don't forgive, you are working for the devil. When you forgive, you are working for God. Who are you working for right now? Who you work for is who you get pay by.

Chapter 3

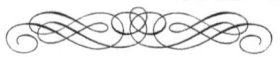

Choices

Life is based upon choices. Choices have automatic benefits or consequences. Our choice determines our destiny to a large extent. Where we are today is based upon the choices we made yesterday or the choices made by those connected to us. Who we will become tomorrow depends on the choices we are making *now*.

Being prayerful before making decisions is wiser and more beneficial than being knowledgeable and hasty. Being careful is more important than being able. If you are not careful in handling a situation, thing, or person, you can ruin something beautiful in the process or even make a situation worse than it was.

Being humble and helpful to others are more important than exalting oneself above others. Always wanting to receive but never giving back is bad practice. Hands that are not useful to its own body and serviceable to others are bad hands.

Do not ignore warnings, red flags, or good advice. They are safety for your future. Ask questions, and investigate a matter. Never make conclusions based upon assumptions and emotions. The results in most cases are wrong. Pay close attention to details.

Some things, some people, some places, some fashions, and some habits are like crazy glue—easy to attach to but hard to break off from. Be mindful of what and who you get attached to. They or it can or will become a blessing or a burden. They or it will push you up or bring you down, give you joy or bring you sorrows.

Association leads to identification. Remember, you *control* your choices no matter how strong the outside influence is. You will have to deal with the results, so always follow your heart and make the right and wise choice.

Good choices make you feel and look good today but cost you a lot tomorrow. Better choices make you feel and look better tomorrow but make and give you less than what you deserve (average). Best choices: you must sacrifice the pleasure and comfort of today to reap the blessings and prosperity of you future.

Decisions must be made based upon producing the results, not based on feelings, pleasure, or comfort. Results are important than choices so prayerfully and wisely consider the end results before you make the choice. Example, when you choose Jesus Christ as your Lord and Savior, obey His voice and Word. The blessings of the Lord rest upon you and remain with you despite your daily challenges. It is never too late to make the right choice. Start now. What you don't care for today, you will pay for tomorrow.

When you ignore warnings and good advice, you will end up paying too much for too little. Time and resources are very limited. You cannot afford to pay high, hard price for temporary little things. Sometimes, what you like is not what you need to succeed. You must be willing to let go of what you like and pursue what you need.

Listen more. Learn faster and change, or else you will stay stuck in your past. DON'T CREATE SOMETHING UNNECESSARY TO DEAL WITH WHEN YOU CAN EASILY AVOID IT.

Wisdom Mixed with Common Sense

Some of the guiding principles that govern my life:

1. Always have faith in God. Never give up. Get back up and keep on fighting, and you will win. Here are some common sayings:

    ➤ "Winners never quit, and quitters never win."
    ➤ "Tough times don't last, but tough people do."
    ➤ "The downfall of a man is not the end of his life."

    Life is too short to have a pity party. Get back up fast. People want to celebrate you and your honest achievements not your pity. Stay focused, and keep pressing forward faster and careful. You will surpass all the requirements and set a new and high standard of success. Determination makes great men and women. Determination will always overcome situations no matter how difficult they are. Only those who dare to try harder again will break the barriers of false limitations placed on their lives.

2. You must be quick to admit when you are wrong and repent so that you can maintain a good conscious. This will enable you to discern between right and wrong at all times. The first step to solving any problem is to admit that there is a problem. Problems are opportunities to become creative and tap into hidden potentials and resources. When you don't admit to existing problems, you miss out on great life changing solutions.

    Learn from your mistakes, and do things differently. Some things, some systems, some people, some organizations, some places, etc. will not change. You will have to change. Change is the essence of life. Anything or anyone who is not changing is not growing. Anything that is not growing is slowly dying. In life, we change from babies to teens, from teens to young adults, from young adults to adults, from adults to elders, and from elders to aged. Making good changes always reveals the better you. Only people who are constantly positively changing can inspire and initiate positive changes in others and their environment. If you do not allow God to begin changing the bad habits or character in you today, you will miss out on the great person you can become tomorrow.

Life is made of constant unavoidable changes from birth to death. Wise people prepare for change, influence change, or initiate change whereas unwise people wait for change, question change, and become a casualty of change. Wake up and change for the better before change isolate you from society. Change is your opportunity to make your tomorrow better than your today.

The things that are relevant today will expire tomorrow. In order to stay relevant, you must keep changing for the better. You've got to be different to make a difference. The difference is what matters. The difference stands out. The difference attracts attention and gain support so find pleasure in being different in a positive way.

You must begin to think, believe, say, and do things different in order to produce a different result.

- What you don't care for today, you will pay for tomorrow. You might end up paying too much for too little.

- Don't create something unnecessary to deal with, when you can easily avoid it.

- Making good changes always reveals the better you.

- The things that are relevant today will expire tomorrow.

- Change is your opportunity to make your tomorrow better than your today.

Chapter 4

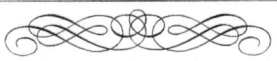

Insight for Youth

You don't have to make a mistake before you come to your senses. Rather, come to your senses before you make a major mistake because some mistakes have an automatic lifetime costly price attached to them.

Sometimes, you cannot see how damaging to the success of your life some mistakes are, until you have to deal with the consequences daily. Today, too many of our young people die early due to bad influence, wrong choices, unfortunate situations, or no or bad parental guidance.

The most important thing on any building is the foundation. The strength or solidity of the foundation determines the capacity and the height of the building. The years of childhood and youth make the foundation of our lives. Your upbringing, parenting, mentoring, culture, values, exposures, beliefs, education, environment, etc. serve as construction materials to build a solid or weak foundation for your life. That is why good parental guidance and proper upbringing is so important. Some parents choose to become the friend of their children instead of being the parent they should.

Some parents refuse to train their children in the right way they should go. Children do not know better. They ought to be taught and trained. Good training is one of the major differences between success and failure. You can always tell the difference in performance and mannerism between a child who is trained and the one who is not. Good training always imposes discipline on the mind and body in preparation to succeed at future task. "Train up a child in the way he should go and when he is old he will not depart from it" (Proverbs 22:6).

Even when a child goes astray, after a while he or she finds out that the grass is not greener on the other side. Actually, they soon discover that it was not green grass but little sharp pebbles painted green on the other side. They quickly return to the convictions of the true values instilled in them from childhood. We are cautioned by the wisest man who lived during his time, King Solomon, in the book of Ecclesiastes 12:1: "Remember now thy creator in the days of thy youth."

Being raised in a home where the Bible is taught and practiced in a balanced way, exposes you to divine wisdom and guidance. Not only that, but it ties you to the most sovereign one who has the power to provide, protect, and lead you victoriously through the storms of life. If a boat is not tied to the dock very well, it drifts away when the ties get high and the storm began to blow. When we connect with God by receiving His Son, Jesus Christ, as our Lord and Savior, it ties us to His ever-abiding presence, which protects and guides us through the storms of life. Through the power of His presence, the storms refine us instead of destroying us as the enemy intended.

> He that dwelled in the secret place of the most high shall abide under the shadow of the almighty. I will say of the LORD He is my refuge and my fortress. My God in Him will I trust. (Psalm 91:1)

Too many of our young people raise themselves. One major contributing factor is the immorality supported and practiced in our society today unashamedly—*kids having kids.*

According to statistics from Family Planning Plus, approximately 750,000 American teens get pregnant every single year resulting in approximately 400,000 teen births. Though it is very damaging to the future of young people, early teenage sexual activities are highly promoted and supported in our society today in all forms and at all levels. This includes many parents, social media, fashion designers, Hollywood, businesses, schools, and government. Instead of being encouraged to abstain for sexual activities, condoms and patches are supplied to teens free of charge.

Sexual immorality has the highest promotion in the secular world. At the same time, sexual misconduct is the fastest way to defame one's character and degrade one's standard and status.

After having sex with a minor, you are charged with statutory rape and must register as a sex offender. If our society would invest more into education, positive creativity, development of special skills and talents, our future will be better. Our future lies in the hearts and hands of our young people of today.

Secondly, according to Wikipedia, youth incarceration in the United States is higher than any other country in the world. In 2010, approximately 70,800 juveniles were incarcerated in youth detention facilities. Approximately 50,000 youth are brought to detention centers in a given year. This does not include juveniles tried as adults.

We have the responsibilities to keep reaching out to our youth with God's *love*, truth, and wisdom because they are tomorrow's leader whether we like it or not. They will lead us upward or downward, backward or forward.

Exit 18 without Proper Preparation

The man who is unprepared never gets the job done effectively. Our society and culture has made it mandatory that our young people take Exit 18 even if they are not mentally, emotionally, morally, financially, socially, or educationally prepared. Many failures, bad choices, disasters, setbacks, etc. that occurred in the lives of many young people, can be contributed to them being exposed to the reality of different levels and phases of life immature and unprepared. The age of eighteen does not mean your mind is prepared to make the decisions of life. Guidance is necessary.

Proper preparation is a necessity for success in life. This was the motto of my English instructor Ms. T. Morgan in middle school: "He who fails to prepare prepares to fail." This motto stayed on the chalkboard, and no one was allowed to erase it. Lack of preparation leads to failure, embarrassment, and sometimes disasters.

Proper preparation is a process that is necessary to produce excellent results. When I was in Bible College, my instructor for systematic theology, Rev. Williamson, had the five *P*s at the top of the chalkboard also: "Proper preparation prevents poor performance."

We must learn to prepare for what we expect, or else our expectation will become an embarrassment when it shows up instead of a blessing. As a youth, it is better and wiser to be prepared before moving from one stage of life to the other.

Today, we live in a microwave, drive-through society. Drive through and get it. The spirit of restlessness has taken over the minds of people. Teenagers are doing everything to look like or become adults overnight, and some adults are doing everything to look like or become a teenager again.

Everything takes time to grow. Anything that grows overnight, ends up dying overnight. Any fruit that gets ripe soon, gets rotten soon, gets forgotten soon. Take time to grow up, young people. Your time on earth is so limited. Material things we accumulate are only valuable for a short season. Enjoy your youth; it is precious. If you do all that adults do while you are young, what will be left for you to do when you become an adult.

Today, many young people always want to have what they see others with, even though they don't know how they got it.

THE STORY IS NEVER TRUE FROM THE OUTSIDE VIEW. Sometimes your life is far better off with the little you have, than the people you see and admire with the fame, fortune, and hidden misery.

"Do not be anxious about anything, but in every situation, by prayer and petition, with thanksgiving, present your request to God" (Philippians 4:6). "But godliness with contentment is great gain" (1 Timothy 6:6).

Boys in Men Bodies and Girls in Women Bodies

The development of your body does not depict the maturity of your mind. Your mind and your spirit are the control center of your decisions and actions. You can have a fully developed body and a very, very immature mind and spirit. This makes you very vulnerable because the ability to comprehend the consequences and benefits of decisions are not in your body but your mind and spirit. Submission to godly counsel and good parental guidance is part of the learning and growing process. This can save you from many costly mistakes.

Life is about perceptions, decisions, actions, and accepting responsibilities. It only takes one decision to change our position in life from worse to better or from better to worse. Many young people are deceived to believe that they are mature because of the development of their bodies. They anxiously expose themselves to things in life that their minds are not yet mature enough to comprehend. Consequently, they make emotional decisions. The results of those decisions are far beyond imagination when the reality sets in. By then, it's too late to reverse.

Things come with time and stage. Wait for your time and stage. All trees do not bear fruits at the same time. Your time is coming sooner than you think. Today, many of our young people trade precious time for temporary things.

While on a prison tour, an inmate asked me for some money. I responded, "I don't have any money." He replied,

"Money makes me high, money is the most valuable thing out there. Gotta get that bread else you won't make it. All I want is money."

By the leading of the Holy Spirit, I said to him, "Money is not the most valuable thing out there, *time is*. What good is the money when you don't have time to spend it with your family, or the people you love, because you are locked up for years behind bars."

Today, many kids are growing up without a positive role model in their lives. What we teach and share with time, can never be taught with things. Time with your family is one of the most valuable things in this world. Don't substitute time with things.

Things gotten at the wrong time by the wrong means, are never happily and peacefully enjoyed. Your deeds always come back to haunt you. In the Bible, it is recorded that the servant of Elisha, Gehazi; lied to get things from Naaman. Naaman was the Captain of the Syrian army. God healed Naaman from the leprosy through His Prophet Elisha. The things he lied to get were cursed things, so he ended up receiving the leprosy Captain Naaman had.

Gehizi was being mentored by Elisha to be a prophet. At the proper time, Gehazi would have had access to all the blessed and good things, but he did not wait for his term. Secondly, not everything and everyone that looks good is blessed and suitable.

> But Elisha said to him, "Was not my spirit with you when the man got down from his chariot to meet you? IS THIS THE TIME to take money or to accept clothes—or olive groves and vineyards, or flocks and herds, or male and female slaves? Naaman's leprosy will cling to you and to your descendants forever." Then Gehazi went from Elisha's presence and his skin was leprous-it became as white as snow. (1 Kings 5:26–27)

Elisha's question to Gehazi "Is this the time?" implied that the timing and the process was wrong. It also emphasizes the need for patience and diligence to acquire the things we desire. My mom always said, "He who laughs last, laughs the best laugh."

It's not what's in your hands that matters most, but what you do with what is in your heart and head. You can have a lot in your hands, but if you have nothing in your heart and head, you will end up losing all that is in your hands. A good example is the story of the prodigal son found the Bible, Matthew 15. He had a lot of inherited material wealth in his hands, but no fear for God in his heart. He lacked self-discipline and wisdom. He loss all his substance to wild living.

Keep the Product Covered

About fifteen years ago, I worked as a floor supervisor/lead for a big company. I had the opportunity to supervise the work of many attractive, talented, and diligent young men and women. There was one young lady whose physical structure and beauty stood out. Most of the young who worked in her section were attracted to her. In addition to her fascinating beauty and structure, she violated the dress code policy regularly. She wore deep V-cut T-shirts, which exposed most of her chest in an indecent manner. She became very popular so fast, it appears that every day the cut in her T-shirt got deeper. As her direct supervisor, it was part of my responsibility to give her a verbal warning followed by a written counseling if she continued violating the dress code policy, which she did. I began to pray and ask God to give me the wisdom as to how to approach the matter, just not to address the violation of the dress code policy but that He would bring a change in her heart concerning her self-image and appearance. This is how the LORD worked so beautifully.

One day she had a problem with the system where she was assigned. She came to me for assistance. Part of my responsibilities was to troubleshoot software and hardware issues in order to keep the system running. That day, I had on my desk two items of the same product. One was in the box, sealed with the plastic covering just as it came from the factory. The other product had a few scratch marks. It had no box because the box had gotten damaged while it was being moved from one location to the other.

The products on my desk got her attention. She said, "I like this product. As soon as I receive my next paycheck, I will buy one." The Holy Spirit used the product to minister to her.

I asked Deve, "When you go to the store to buy this item, will you buy the one used as a sample out of the box, or will you buy the new one in the box sealed with the plastic from the factory?"

She responded, "That's a dumb question, Mr. Flowers." She continued, "No one buys the product that is out of the box."

I asked, "Why not?"

She said, "It has collected dirt. Everyone touches it with their dirty hands and tests it to see how it works. That's why it is called a sample." She concluded by saying, "Without the box wrapping or cover, the product loses half of its value. Any buyer can bargain to pay half price or less."

I commended Ms. Deve by saying, "You have spoken nothing but the truth. You are very knowledgeable in marketing."

She smile brightly back at me.

Then I said, "Ms. Deve, you just told me that no one buys the product that is outside the box, and if they do, they only pay half price or less."

She confirmed, "That is the truth, ask anyone."

I said, "I believe you. That's why I'm seizing this moment to ask you going forward, please keep the product covered."

She said, "Which product?"

I said, "That one," referring to her chest, which was almost completely outside the deep V-cut and ripped T-shirt. I said, "As you know, it is against the dress code policy. You should have gotten a write-up long time ago, but God just doesn't want us to change our clothes. He wants to change our hearts, our mind-set, and our ways." From that day, Deve never wore another deep V-cut T-shirt to work. She thanked me for the enlightenment and promised to carry herself better.

- ✓ Covering is protection from external pollution or danger.
- ✓ Everything and everyone of high value and importance are protected by covering.
- ✓ Covering attracts respect and proper approach.

The presidents, kings, and queens of nations, movie stars, pop stars, athlete, rich and wealthy people, and others are constantly covered by tight security agents because of their importance. All military and security officers wear bulletproof vests to cover their vital internal organs because of their importance to their lives. Expensive vehicles are kept in closed garages. Treasures, jewelries, monies of large quantity are kept in coded safe because of the value. Anything of value, demands to be covered for its protection and durability.

Lust

Lust is highly promoted today. Lust always leads to destructive end because lust is self-centered. The lust of the eyes and flesh drive people impatiently after material things and sexual *gratification*.

> For all that is in the world, the lust of the flesh, the lust of the eyes, and the pride of life, is not of the Father, but is of the world.

> And the world passed away and the lust thereof; but he that doeth the will of God abideth forever. (1 John 2:16–17)

> Flee also youthful lusts: but follow righteousness, faith, charity, peace, with them that call on the Lord out of a pure heart. (2 Timothy 2:22)

Lust is attracted to the body, but pure love is attracted to the heart. The spirit of lust causes us to chase after the physical structure (bodies) or material things of people with a selfish desire to gratify our sexual and material appetite.

It is highly possible to become intimate with a man or woman whose heart is fully connected with someone else. Eventually, their bodies will follow where their heart is. Love is based upon nothing else but love. Love goes beyond physical structure and material things. It seeks to win the heart, not just the body for sexual pleasure. Today's latest fashion is called *naked*.

The more naked or less covering you wear, the more popular you become on the entertainment red carpet, the more money you are paid by Hollywood, *Playboy* magazine, and others. Modesty and moral values are going down the drain fast in the jet plane of today's culture of "no wrongs, all rights" and "it's okay." Perversion is sweeping the hearts of men and women like a tornado. What a shame.

Young people, I am not saying be old-fashioned in your appearance, but there should be a limit in exposing the private parts of your body publicly. Set a high moral standard for yourself. Good looks and things do not determine someone's character.

Our bodies are the house of our spirit and soul. Each human body housed a good spirit and soul or a bad spirit and soul. You cannot tell the character of the spirit or soul by the attraction from the beauty or structure of a human body.

The body attracts but it is a good spirit and soul that make good relationship, keeps good relationship and advances good relationship.

Good ways have greater and lasting impact than good looks. The crowd is not always right. When you know who you are, you don't follow the crowd.

Not every fashion suits everyone. Be modest in your choice of clothing. A little exposure creates curiosity of good interest; whereas, over exposure attracts no curiosity of interest because everything is already seen.

Image is everything. Due to the stereotypical system of our society, you are judged by your appearance even before you are spoken to or before people even find out who you really are. There is never a second chance to make a first impression. Your first impression is a lasting impression. What the eyes see stick longer than what the ears hear and the mind reads. You must learn to look your best at all times. Someone is always watching that you don't see. They look up to you as role model. Secondly, you could run into a person of affluence, who could assist you, meet your goals or fulfill your vision. They could be easily turned off by your appearance and misjudge you.

Seductive attires sometimes lead to sexual attraction and predators. According to the "victims of sexual violence" statistics, on average, there are 321,500 victims (age twelve or older, majority under thirty) of rape and sexual assault each year in the United States.

Younger people are at the highest risk of sexual violence: 82 percent of all juvenile are female, and 90 percent of adult rape victims are female. According to RAINN report: females ages sixteen to nineteen are four times more likely than the general population to be victims of rape. Women ages eighteen to twenty-four who are college students are three times more likely than women in general to experience sexual assault; 11.2% of all students experience rape or sexual assault through physical force, violence, or incapacitation among all graduate and undergraduate students. College-age victims of sexual violence often do not report to law enforcement. Students are at an increased risk during the first few months of their first and second semesters in college.

Bottom line is, we live in a perverted, immoral, ungodly, demonically influenced world. We must help our young people protect themselves as much as possible. Most people work hard for years and years to earn what they have and become who they are. That is wonderful and a good example for all to follow.

On the other hand, some of the hard-code criminals and prostitutes have the most well-defined and beautiful bodies. Some criminals devote all the time locked up in prison to all types of physical exercise, which is a good thing health-wise. Most criminals commit crime to have access to a lot of money. Money gives them options to live in the best homes, ride the best cars, have the best health care, have the best surgeons to perform any type of plastic surgery to make them look the best, etc. Make no mistake, some criminals are good people because some people are WRONGFULLY CHARGED AND IMPRISONED.

The point I want to emphasize is that if you only claim that you love someone because they have a nice body structure and nice things, you could end up falling in love with a son or daughter of the devil. It is highly possible for a person to have a beautiful body, nice things, and a very wicked, self-centered heart.

I believe the TV show *Dating Naked* is so wrong and one of the poorest example of initiating or developing a healthy love relationship because the beauty and physical definition of a person's body tell you nothing about their character. It only invites the spirit of lust to take over your mind. Character makes a man and a woman, not looks.

God is *love*. God never deals with us base upon our outward appearance or material possessions. He deals with us strictly based upon our heart. Life and love are in the heart. When the heart ceases to beat, life is over.

> But the LORD said unto Samuel, Look not on his countenance, or on the height of his stature; because I have refused him: for the LORD sees not as man sees: for man looks on the outward appearance, but the LORD looks on the heart. (1 Samuel 16:7)

Love from the heart is what matters, because physical structure can have a deformity or physical breakdown anytime; due to incidents or accidents in life. *Some* men and *some* women have bodies that are like beautiful empty containers. They are attractive on the outside, but they have no substance or character on the inside. Their outside draws your attention close to them, but their character/behavior runs you a million miles away from them. Empty container makes a lot of noise. They talk a lot and do a little. They lack wisdom and understanding. Their looks are their password. When you take away their looks, you are left with unexpected continuous problems.

It is possible for a person to have a nice body and a wicked heart and a stubborn, easily angry, insecure and lazy spirit hidden inside. Also, you can have a not-so-well defined body and a loving, sweet, gentle, understanding, hardworking , humble, and God-fearing spirit hidden inside.

That is why, it is wise to take time to be just friends before you become lovers. Time and observance will teach you a lot about people without you paying a penny. Stop allowing your heart to be broken or spirit to be wounded by chasing empty beautiful or handsome containers—good looks, sweet talk, but no character. Your relationship with others should be a blessing and not a burden and vice versa.

Again, pay close attention to red flags in people's characters. Don't be deceived. You cannot change another person's character. Only God can change a person's heart. Be mindful of the type of spirit you open yourself to. You can open yourself to the evil of an unclean spirit in another person by opening your heart to them without physical contact. "Keep your heart with all diligence; for out of it are the issues of life" (Proverbs 4:23).

It is best to discover the mind-set of a person by listening to them more, and talking when necessary; before you let them into your heart. A man's or woman's actions are controlled by their mind-set. Their mind-set is controlled by what's in their heart, what they hear, and what they see with your eyes. It is wiser to discontinue friendship with someone than to commit yourself to a love relationship with them hoping that they will change. You will be very disappointed because they won't change.

- ✓ Never give yourself to someone who does not know your value and purpose. They will treat you like trash. They will use you and misuse you.
- ✓ Too many people are hurt in relationship or stuck with their nightmare all because they chose to ignore the red flags in the character of the other person.
- ✓ No one is perfect, but you deserve someone suitable. Someone with less issues is far better than someone with major life problems. You will have to deal with those problems all your life. Sometimes it causes you to be unhappy in your relationship. You don't want a relationship out of sympathy or desperation but out of genuine love. You deserve to be loved and respected.
- ✓ God only blesses what God accepts, and God only accepts what God prescribes. God prescribed marriage to consist of a union between one man and one woman.

CAN GOD MAKE MISTAKES? NO. No matter which sex you choose to be medically, physically, and immorally changed into for your pleasure, no one can change your spirit and soul, which is eternal. Where will your soul spend eternity after this short stay on earth? God loves everyone, but God has standards and requirements in order to spend eternity with Him.

Receive God's love through His Son, Jesus Christ, and follow His ways. The Bible is your guidelines. Jesus never rejects or condemns us regardless of our sins. He forgives us when we repent and shows us the way out of every bondage.

Drug Usage and Overdose

Today our society promotes the use of elusive drugs. According to the NIDA, about 570,000 people die annually in the US due to drug use. More than 480,000 deaths related to tobacco, about 31,000 due to alcohol, nearly 22,000 due to overdose from illicit (illegal) drugs, and close to 23,000 due to overdose from prescription pain relievers.

National overdose deaths: 15,000 males and 10,000 females died in 2015 from OD. This number is rapidly increasing. Drug overdose rate among youth and young adult triple every year. Marijuana use is widespread in schools, especially among tenth grade to twelfth grade. Statistics shows that the frequent use of marijuana leads to a stronger desire for more potent drugs. Many of our young people at wide parties mix drugs and alcohol, which in most cases lead to overdose, rape, violence, vandalism, etc.

A little bit leads to a little more, and a little more leads to addiction. Say no the first time, and you won't have to worry about the second. You have the right to be uncommon. Drug use, gun violence, sex out of marriage, assorted crimes, etc. are highly promoted at all levels in our society today, especially through the media, music, culture, government, communities, etc. Choose not to be an experiment for drug promotions etc, by any of these entities.

The spirit of contentment, patience, and respect for others' rights has been driven out of many people's hearts. Some people are no longer humble and contented with what they have been blessed with. They want more at all cost. Some parents even trade time with their children for promotion on the job or accumulation of more expensive things.

Things can never replace time. With time, you can establish a close bond and teach your children many valuable things. You cannot do that by buying more stuff. Some kids leave a home full of expensive toys and go hunting for a friend who can give them love, attention, and a listening ear. In most cases, they choose the wrong people as friends who introduce them to the wrong things, places, and people.

You can have a house full of stuff but very empty of genuine love, attention, playtime, correction, fun time, healthy meals, prayer time, and good relationship. The most valuable things in a home are not tangible, such as peace, respect, love, forgiveness, understanding, right choice of words and tone of voice, reasoning, etc.

Who Sees Further

I was in the cafeteria of my workplace, having lunch. Sitting at the table opposite me was an angry-looking young lady sitting all by herself. I was led to reach out to her, so I asked her permission to sit at the table with her. Her response was "I don't care," so I sat. I said, "It appears like something must be bothering you." She lashed out, "It's my mom. She doesn't like my boyfriend. She doesn't like the way he dresses. She doesn't like for me to hang out late. She's trying to control my life. She doesn't like ..." Blah, blah, blah, blah, and she went on, and I just listened.

At the end of her venting, I asked her how old she was. She forcefully responded "Eighteen, which meant I'm old enough to make my own decisions." Then I asked her how old her mom was. She said. "Forty-two years old."

I said, "Do you mind playing a game with me?"

She said, "I don't feeling like playing no game with you, sir. You don't understand. My mom is getting on my last nerves, and I am about to get my own place and move out with my boyfriend."

I said, "It's only a two-minute imaginary game, and this is how it goes: Imagine you and your mom are in a very tall building with fifty floors. You are on the eighteenth floor, and she is on the forty-second floor. Now, let's take an imaginary walk to the windows and look outside. Tell me who sees further."

She said, "What do you mean?"

I said, "Both of you are looking at the outside world from where you are. Just tell me who sees further down the road."

She said, "Obviously, she sees further because she's higher on the forty-second floor."

I said, "Sandra, that's the point. Your mom sees further. She sees things that you will never see and understand until you are forty-two years old. She doesn't hate you, she's trying to guide you with good advice and show you the right way to go. She sees beyond what you can see at eighteen. She sees the traps, the deceptions, the road blocks down the block that you cannot see from the eighteenth floor. One day when you reach the age of forty-two, it will all make sense to you, and you will thank her for her wisdom, protection, and guidance, which you don't understand now."

Sandra got so quiet. She said, "Thank you, and I apologize for being rude to you. I never saw it that way. I will make up with my mom and listen to her more."

Young people, listen to good advice. It will save you from continuous trouble. Stop saying "I don't care." You should care because what you don't care for today, you will pay for tomorrow. You might end up paying too much for too little.

- Proper preparation is a process that is necessary to produce excellent results.

- Any fruit that gets ripe soon, gets rotten soon, gets forgotten soon. Nothing and no one grows overnight. Real blessings come with time and stage.

- All trees don't bear fruits at the same time.

- Wait for your time and wear your size. It fits and look good.

- Proper preparation prevents poor performance.

- Everything takes time to grow. Anything that grows overnight, ends up dying overnight. Any fruit that gets ripe soon, gets rotten soon, gets forgotten soon.

- Take time to grow up, young people. Enjoy your youth; it is precious.

- The story is never true from the outside view.

- Life is about perceptions, decisions, accepting responsibilities, and taking initiatives.

- Good ways have greater and lasting impact than good looks, so change your ways for the better.

- You deserve to be loved purely and respected highly.

- Things can never replace time.

- With time, you can establish a close bond and teach your children many valuable things. You cannot do that by buying more stuff.

- The most valuable things in a home are not tangible, such as caring, peace, respect, love, forgiveness, understanding, right choice of words and tone of voice, reasoning, etc.

- Boys in men bodies and girls in women bodies. The maturity of your body has nothing to do with the maturity of your mind. Your mind should control your life not your body.

- Seek good guidance, listen and apply it.

- The attractive structure of your body has nothing to do with the integrity of your reputation or good character. Body attracts but good character keeps.

- Good behavior has greater positive impact than good looks.

- It only takes one decision to change our position in life from worse to better or from better to worse.

- All trees do not bear fruits at the same time. Wait, be contented, your time is coming soon.

Chapter 5

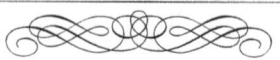

Three Ms: Mind, Mouth, Movements

Equal Your Destiny

In order to succeed at anything, you must consistently align your mind, mouth, and movements in the same direction. This means, you have to consistently say what you think and do what you say. The soundness of your mind is the power of great actions. Numerous verses in the Bible cautioned believers to maintain a sober mind. Below are a few of those references:
But the end of all things is at hand: be ye therefore sober, and watch unto prayer. (1 Peter 4:7)

Be sober, be vigilant; because your adversary the devil, as a roaring lion, walketh about, seeking whom he may devour. (1 Peter 5:8)

Believers are warned to be sober because the one thing their adversary, the devil, wants from them is to control their minds. If the devil can gain control of your mind, he is in control of everything you say and do.

One means by which believers can help to maintain a sober mind, is to avoid the influence of things and people who will dilute their faith in Jesus Christ. To be drunk means to lose soundness of mind. When you lose soundness of mind, you lose your ability to win battles and to overcome situations. When you lose soundness of mind, you become a prey to your enemies and situations. Alcohol is not the only substance that can make a man or woman drunk. It's possible to become drunk with power, fame, position, talents, materialism, beauty, sex, wealth, etc.

Your mind is the control center of your actions. What you put in your mind comes out through your decisions and actions. Whoever or whatever controls your mind controls your life. A man is not free until he is freed in his mind. That is why even if a man or a woman is taken out of a physical prison, if he or she is a not delivered from prison mentality, though free, he or she will still behave as if they were still imprisoned.

All victories and defeat in the battles of life situations and circumstances, are won or lost first in our mind before they happen in real life. Our greatest asset is our mind. With our mind, we can give birth to a new beautiful beginning despite an ugly past. All things are created twice—first in our minds and second by our actions. Therefore, we can create a good, new future by embracing new thoughts and taking new actions. All transformation into a better or worse person or destination is first birthed in the mind and accomplished by our actions.

When we think small, we act small and ask for small things. When we think big, we act big, and we ask for big things. We are the sum total of our thoughts and the multiplication of our actions. Our thoughts control our decisions, and our actions determine our results to a large extent. "For as he thinketh in his heart, so is he" (Proverbs 23:7a).

Good and pure thoughts lead to good and pure deeds. Bad and dirty thoughts lead to bad and dirty actions. We cannot control the thoughts that come to our mind at times, but we can always control the thoughts that stay on our mind. Since our thoughts control our action, when thoughts are good, we should meditate on it. When thoughts are wrong or evil, we should replace them fast with godly, positive, and good thoughts.

> Finally, brethren, whatsoever things are true, whatsoever thing are honest, whatsoever things are just, whatsoever things are pure, whatsoever things are lovely, whatsoever things are of good report; if there be any virtue, and if there be any praise, think on these things. (Philippians 4:8)

As Christians, we are encouraged to develop and maintain a mind like Jesus Christ so we can speak and act like Christ did. "Let this mind be in you, which was also in Christ Jesus" (Philippians 2:5). Christ had a mind that was submitted to the will, plan, and purpose of His father. "And he went a little further, and fell on his face, and prayed, saying, O my Father, if it be possible, let this cup pass from me: nevertheless not as I will, but thou will" (Matthew 26:39).

Christ was mission-minded. His mission was to save mankind by sacrificing His life on the cross of Calvary. When you are on a mission, your feelings and comfort are not important. Accomplishing your mission is most important. Many people do not fulfill their mission or become the best in their field because they are easily distracted, or they try to do too many things at the same time. Therefore, they are unable to invest the quality of time and work required to be the best or to finish what they started. Accomplishing great things demand that you become single-minded.

Consistently focus and press relentlessly toward the goal set before you. Don't stop until the task is completed well. No matter what it cost, keep going, keep doing, and keep pressing harder. The harder you press, the closer you get to the finish line of great accomplishment, joy, and celebration. Sometimes, taking breaks or days and weeks off from your goals or vision brings in discouragement, setback, loss of support, loss of enthusiasm, loss of zeal, and the loss of everything you invested the first time you started.

You must focus like you are driving in the tunnel. There are only two things you can do when driving through the tunnel—that is to look ahead and keep driving forward. Never stop while driving in the tunnel. It will cause major delays or, even worse, major accidents. From my experience, the number-one rule to apply when running is to keep running despite how you feel. The number-two rule to apply is never stop. Run in place until your path is clear, and keep running toward your target. The number-three rule is just before you reach your finish line, set a new target and keep running. Dream another dream, reach further, press harder, run faster, and set a higher standard for yourself.

Look ahead, and keep driving forward. Don't just be anybody; be the best body.

Keep Your Spiritual Mind Sight above Your Natural Eyesight and Mind-Set

In the Bible, the book of Genesis 13:14–16 teaches a profound lesson about seeing the beauty and greatness of your future with the eyes of your understanding.

> And the LORD said unto Abram, after that Lot was separated from him, Lift up now thine eyes, and look from the place where thou art northward, and southward, and eastward, and westward: For all the land which thou seest, to thee will I give it, and to thy seed forever. And I will make thy seed as the dust of the earth: so that if a man can number the

dust of the earth, then shall thy seed also be numbered. (Genesis 13:14–16)

Insights from the Above Scripture

Sometimes you have to prayerfully and wisely separate or disconnect from things, places, and people that serve as a hindrance to your well-being and the success of your future. God only gave Abram a winning strategy and a vision of his glorious future after he was separated from his nephew Lot. According to Genesis 13:1–10, Abraham became very wealthy in livestock, silver, and gold as God blessed him. There was confusion and division between Abram's herders and Lot's herders. Lot and his men were envious of Abram's accumulating wealth, so they started quarreling.

Not everyone can stand to see you accumulate massive wealth because of your sacrificial private obedience to God without wealth. Not everyone you like you can trust for your well-being. Some folks will betray you in split seconds for material things, position, or a new friend.

Abraham was very concerned about who will inherit the massive wealth God was blessing him with, because he was childless. God visited Abraham in a vision according to the Bible in the book of Genesis chapter 15:1–6.

> And he brought him forth abroad, and said, Look now toward heaven, and tell the stars, if thou be able to number them: and he said unto him, so shall thy see be. And he believed the LORD; and he counted it to him for righteousness. (Genesis 15:5–6)

In the above reference, God showed Abraham a physical picture of the uncountable stars in the heaven as a symbol of what his future would be like, even though it contradicted the reality of his condition at the time.

A mental picture of your future, which is a vision, transformed into a physical picture (which can be in the form of a written plan, painting on a paper or board, diagram, statue, sculpture, a drawing, or picture taken, etc.) will eventually lead to the actualization of its reality. See the glory of your future through the lenses of your imaginations and not lenses of your past or present circumstances.

Paint, draw, or write every aspect of your future on a paper or board as God shows it to you. Place it on a wall where you can see it every day, and meditate upon it and see yourself in it or with it. Pray for direction and resources to accomplish it day and night. Write down a step by step flexible plan as to show how you intend to accomplish your goal or vision. God will give wisdom, direction, connection and favor with the right people who can help you. Pursue it with all you got. God will make it a reality.

Years ago in the nineties, I served as financial assistant for World Vision International located in Monrovia. An elderly man called Mr. Wallace from an area called Caldwell also served WVI at the time as the maintenance man. In his private life, he was an artist. He carved little jet planes and other objects out of wood. I was impressed by his work, so I asked him to carve me two jet planes of the same size and paint them white. The order was completed and paid for. The planes looked as good as the real ones even though no one could fly them. I brought the jet planes home and placed them on top of the headboard of my bed. Each day I saw myself flying around the world, preaching God's word long before it became a reality. A physical picture of your future goal keeps you focused, passionate, and keep you driving toward it.

Your mind sight sees further than your eyesight. Keep your mind sight above your eyesight and mind-set. Use your imagination to see the accomplishment of your beautiful, glorious future for your natural eyes sight is very limited. God's strategy to Abram was for him to lift the eyes of his understanding above his present condition and location and imagine an unlimited glorious future. Lifted eyes always see possibilities and successful results at the beginning; whereas, natural eyes see obstacles, difficulties, the burden of long processes, and failures. Your mind sight is unlimited, but your eyesight is very limited.

In Genesis 22:4 it says, "Then on the third day Abraham lifted up his eyes, and saw the place afar off." Until you lift up the eyes of your understanding, which is your imagination, you will not see the invisible glorious place God is taking you. Stop looking down on yourself. Your condition is never your conclusion. Stop allowing your history to control your mindset and daily conversation. Thank God, life is made out of a series of changes from birth to death, so you don't have to relive your past. Initiate the changes in your days and years ahead by using your imaginations to design a new and beautiful future. God wants to make your godly imaginations today your reality tomorrow. "Now to Him who is able to do immeasurably more than all we ask or imagine, according to His power that is at work within us." Ephesians 3:20 (NIV)

"Lift up your eyes O ye gates, and be ye lifted up, ye everlasting doors; and the King of Glory shall come in. 8. Who is the King of Glory? The LORD strong and mighty, the LORD mighty in battle" (Psalm 24:7–8).

Only when the eyes of your understanding are lifted up above your situation, the King of Glory comes in with strength, deliverance, and victory. You can only go or progress in the direction you are looking and seeing. When you look or see up, you put your mind in an upward thinking position. You climb and go up. When you look or see down, you put your mind in a downward thinking position. You stumble and fall down. When you look forward, you put your mind in a forward thinking position or motion. You walk, run, drive, or leap forward. When you look backward, you put your mind in a backward thinking motion or position. You reverse, you regress, you go backward, and sometimes you have major accidents because the light is green at this moment, indicating that you go forward. Your situation is a distraction to prevent you from looking up to God for the help you need.

When you head in the wrong direction, you will always have incidents, accidents, and long delays to fulfilling your purpose and reaching your divine destination. When you look in God's direction, you will see your blessings flowing. When you stay in God's direction, you will keep your blessings flowing.

In God's direction you will find His provision and protection. That is why seeing with the eyes of your understanding is so important. Are you heading in the right direction? No matter where you are going or what you desire to accomplish, you must head in the right direction in order to arrive at your desired destination.

Seeing with the mind of your understanding is knowing that you have what you have seen. You have to see yourself as it or with it before you can become it or possess it. Therefore, see yourself happy, healthy, and wealthy. See yourself at the top, winning every battle and overcoming every obstacle. See yourself as God sees you—peculiar, royal priesthood, holy nation, bold, confident, and the apple of his eye. See yourself as a great person achieving great things.

"Keep me as the apple of the eye, hide me under the shadow of thy wings" (Psalm 17:8). "But you are a chosen generation, a royal priesthood, an holy nation, a peculiar people, that ye should shew forth the praises of Him who hath called you out of darkness into his marvelous light" (1 Peter 2:9). In the Bible, the book of Ephesians chapter 1:18, Apostle Paul prays for the enlightening of the believers eyes of understanding.

"The eyes of your understanding being enlightened; that ye MAY KNOW what is the hope of his calling, and what is the riches of the glory of his inheritance in the saints" (Ephesians 1:18). Abram's future was determined by how far he could see himself with the mind of His understanding despite the odds of his condition and location.

How far and how high we see ourselves determines how high we ascend, how wide we expand, and how far we extend.

How Far and How High Do You See Yourself?

Sacred: The closer you draw toward God, the clearer you see because He is the perfect light. Jesus is *the way* to all genuine fulfillment of purpose, success, and prosperity. The higher you press toward God and His things, the further you see because He is the highest of all the highest. He is above all.

> Jesus saith unto him, I am the way, the truth, and the life: no man cometh unto the Father, but by me. (John 14:6)

> This then is the message which we have heard of him, and declare unto you, that God is light, and in him is no darkness at all. (John 1:5)

Abram's strategy from God:

1. Lift the eyes of his understanding above his condition, situation, and location.
2. Look very far into the future.
3. See (imagine) without limitations.

God promised to give Abram only what he saw with the eyes of his understanding. God is committed to speedily deliver what you see with the mind of your understanding according to His plan, timing, and purpose.

> See, I have this day set thee over the nations and over the kingdoms, to root out, and to pull down, and to destroy, and to throw

> down, and to build, and to plant. Moreover the word of the LORD came unto me, saying, Jeremiah, what seest thou? I said, I see a rod of an almond tree. Then said the LORD unto me, thou hast well seen: for I will hasten my word to perform it. (Jeremiah 1:10–12)

Spiritual blindness is the worst condition any believer can be in.

> And they came to Jericho: and as he went out of Jericho with his disciples and a great number of people, blind Bartimaeus, the son of Timaeus, sat by the highway side begging. (Mark 10:46)

From the above scripture reference, we can conclude that blindness made Bartimaeus a sitter (stagnant) and a beggar (dependent on the mercy of others to survive). He asked Jesus for the most important thing, the restoration of his sight. The restoration of his sight broke the circle of limitations over his life. He could see how to do things for himself, move forward instead of being carried. He could see how to prosper. It is possible to have good physical sight, 20/20 vision, and still be spiritually blind.

The enlightening of your eyes of understanding will break the circle of limitations over every aspect of your life and ministry. The real things that are yet to come, are never seen with the physical eyes first; but with the eyes of our understanding which is revealed knowledge (revelation). The eyes of your understanding see the creation and completion of things in the invisible realm, long before they are accomplished in the physical world.

All things are created and accomplished twice. First in the mind, then in the physical by our plans and timely action. Every building and every blessing has an entry point. That entry point could be in the form of a door, a connection or conversation with someone, a position, a gift, a talent or skill, an action or reaction, a decision, a relocation, an act of kindness, a place, or relationship. However, if you are spiritually blind to your entry point or door into your blessings and the timing, you will remain stagnant and begging.

Every blessing, every business, and every opportunity has an opening and closing hours. That is why seeing your point of entry and entering on time is very important. Naturally, we do not see before us because we have good eyesight. We see inside a building because the electric light is on. We see outside because the sunlight is shining. If the lights are turn completely off, and you are in a very dark room with your eyes wide opened, you won't be able to see your hands if you were to wave it before your face. The truth of the matter is, our sight around us and our sight ahead of us depends on the presence of shining lights. Spiritually, light is a representation of revealed knowledge.

A good example of spiritual sight and timely entry is demonstrated in the story in Bible about the woman with the twelve years' issue of blood. This story is recorded in the book of Mark 5:25–34. "For she said, if I may touch but his clothes, I shall be whole" (Mark 5:28).

Insights

    A. She never lost hope even though she had been dealing with her problem for twelve years. Every hospital and doctor she visited had robbed her of her resources but could not give her any cure for her disease.

    B. She saw herself healed with the eyes of her understanding before she was physically healed. She saw Jesus as her healer and the hem of his garment as her entry point to contact or enter that healing power.

    C. She replaced twelve years' history of negative experience with a new mind-set: she said to herself (talking

in her head), if I touch the hem of His garment, I will be made whole.
D. She went after what she saw with the mind of her understanding, and it became a reality in her life.
E. Her new mind sight brought new things to her life.
F. There were other sick people in the same crowd who rubbed against Jesus himself and still remained sick because they were spiritually blind to who he is and what he carried.
G. We must learn to believe in God's possibilities and not our inabilities.

Believe in the impossible, and God will make it happen for you. The wisdom of silent thoughts always produces a far better outcome than instant emotional reaction. We must stop, think, see, and pursue new beneficial outcomes.

You must get a new mind sight about you and your future, if you desire things to change for the better in your life. God's mind sight is the best mind-set to develop because it keeps getting better and better and better.

Every change for the better in a believer's life starts with a new heart, which comes from God by faith, and a new mind-set, which comes from replacing your old mind-set with His Word.

"A new heart also will I give you, and a new spirit will I put within you: and I will take away the stony heart out of your flesh, and I will give you an heart of flesh" (Ezekiel 36:26).

"And be not conformed to this world: but be ye transform by the renewing of your mind, that ye may prove what is that good, and acceptable, and perfect, will of God" (Romans 12:2).

Your ears are double windows to your mind, and your eyes are double doors to your mind. Some of the ways in which we can maintain a sound mind is by avoiding wrong company, and looking straight ahead or, may I say, avoiding attractive distractions. Be mindful of what you allow your ears to hear and what you allow your eyes to constantly watch.

Be not deceived: evil communications corrupt good manners. (1 Corinthians 15:33)

Blessed is the man that walketh not in the counsel of the ungodly, nor standeth in the way of sinners, nor sitteth in the seat of the scornful. (Psalm 1:1)

Let thine eyes look right on, and let thine eyelids look straight before thee. (Proverbs 4:25)

The eye is the light of the whole body.

Because you have rejected knowledge,
I also reject you as my priests;
because you have ignored the law of your God,
I also will ignore your children.
(Hosea 4:6, NIV)

Spiritually, knowledge represents light and light represents revealed knowledge. As light shows you the right way forward, so does knowledge shows you the ways forward and ahead.

You word is a lamp for my feet,
A light on my path.
(Psalms 119:105)

Mouth

Spoken words are the only distinction between human being and other creatures. Words control and express the motion and emotions of all living and nonliving beings. All things are formed and done by words. Our spoken words form our living world. Most of what has occurred in your life over the years are things you thought and spoke consistently.

Spirit-filled spoken words have both creative and destructive supernatural power. Without communication, you are locked up in the prison of loneliness and isolated from the rest of the world. Man is a speaking spirit made in the image and likeness of God. Everything God created, He spoke it into existence. Most of the miracles Jesus performed, He spoke it into existence. Every situation Jesus encountered, He resolved them with faith-filled words. Man must also speak the things he needs or wants into existence like God did.

"For by your words you shall be justified and by your words you shall be condemned" (Matthew 12:37).

You must consistently speak what God says about you, no matter what others think or say the reality is. All living and nonliving things listen and obey God's Word. Speak His Word, and you will see results because God backs His Word. "So shall my word be that goeth forth out of my mouth; it shall not return unto me void, but it shall accomplish that which I please, and it shall prosper in the thing whereto I sent it" (Isaiah 55:11).

You must boldly declare what you want to see happen as the spirit of God leads you. "Thou shalt also decree a thing, and it shall be established unto thee: and the light shall shine upon thy ways" (Job 22:28).

When you go to the store, the sales representative only tells you and gives you what you ask for. When you go to the restaurant, the waitress only brings you what you ordered. If you don't order anything, they won't bring you anything. You must communicate what you see or envision or dream with people who have your best interest at heart.

Understanding the supernatural power attached to spirit-filled words, you must speak against obstacles and hindrances in your life and command them to leave immediately, or else they will stay. There are demonic spirits that control some obstacles and hindrances. Until you bind them and cast them out violently, they will remain.

In the same way, the blessings and promises of God you desire to manifest in your life, you must call forth with authority in the name of Jesus.

> For verily I say unto you, that whosoever shall say unto this mountain, Be thou removed, and be thou cast into the sea; and shall not doubt in his heart, but shall believe that those things which he saith shall come to pass; he shall have whatsoever he saith. (Mark 11:23)

> Death and life are in the power of the tongue and they that love it shall eat the fruit thereof. (Proverbs 18:21)

Every time you open your mouth, you are either speaking life or death over your life and situation. Your spirit-filled words have the power to create what you desire, justify your rights to access your inheritance in Christ, build up what God has given or teardown and remove what God has not promised you.

> Then the Lord put forth His hand and touched my mouth. And the LORD said unto me, Behold, I have put my words in thy mouth. See, I have this day set thee over the nations and over the kingdoms, to root out and to pull down and to destroy, and throw down, to build and to plant. (Jeremiah 1:9–10)

> For by thy words thou shall be justified and by thy words thou shall be condemned. (Matthew 12:37)

It's all about your spirit-filled words. Your words will qualify or disqualify you. Your words will justify or condemn you. Stop using your mouth against yourself. Stop talking about your negative past experience unless you are *led* by God's Spirit to share your testimony to show how much God has done in your life. You must be led to share your negative past experience. Not everyone who listens to your negative past experience, will still respect you and give the same level of acceptance they had for you, before they got to know about your past; because of their lack of spiritual maturity. Some will even go to the extent to deny you opportunities, even though you have been delivered from that form of lifestyle. The key is: be led when to speak, where to speak, and who to share your testimony with. Your testimony will always be uplifting and encouraging.

> Wherefore, my dear brothers and sisters, take note of this: Everyone should be quick to listen, slow to speak and slow to become angry. (James 1:19 (NIV)

> He that keepeth his mouth keepeth his life: but he that openeth wide his lips shall have destruction. (Proverbs 13:3 KJV)

Spirit-Led Timely Movements

Go at once. Great results are products of the demonstration of God's power, sound thoughts, spirit-led timely movements, teamwork and hard work.

No actions, no results. Move faster. GPS is only useful to moving objects and people. Spirit-led movement is proof that you are alive in Christ. Too much physical rest is for the dead. It is usually said, "May your soul rest in peace when you are dead." You must understand that God is at *work* in and through you. "For it is God which worketh in you both to will and do of his good pleasure" (Philippians 2:13).

Your laziness and excuses can slow down or hinder what God wants to get done on time in and through you. Too many breaks sometimes break things up. Stay focused, and be consistent. "Now unto him that is able to do exceeding abundantly above all we can ask or think, according to the power that worketh in us" (Ephesians 3:20). Great accomplishments demand timely right actions.

> Only the Holy Spirit knows your blessings' manifestation timing. Therefore, obey divine signals with a sense of urgency so you can step into the arrangements made by heaven on your behalf.
> Learn to act on time.

When God speaks to you to do something, He has already spoken in advance to everything and everybody else needed to make what He told you become a reality. As you obey God fully, you will discover His unlimited, awaiting, hidden resources needed for every stage of the process of fulfillment.

Every living human being, rich or poor, big or small, educated or uneducated, regardless of your geographical location or status in life, has direct access to twenty-four hours every day. Everyone has equal amount of time every day. You can choose to invest your time in the right things to produce quality results, or you can waste your precious time behind things and people that will keep your life stagnant. Where you invest your time, is where you will see results.

Every blessing, every business, and every opportunity has opening and closing hours. That is why seeing your point of entry and entering on time is very important.

"And the LORD answered me and said: write the vision and make it plain on tables, that he may RUN that readeth it" (Habakkuk 2:2).

Plan ahead and prepare to make your plan a successful reality.

a) Writing your vision on paper prepares you for timely right actions.
b) It also enables you to have it handy to share with the right people who can support it.
c) It gives you the opportunity to review it constantly and be more creative.

God is a prepared God, and he deals with prepared people. Expectation without preparation equals embarrassment. The future belongs to faster accurate runners, not sitters, not walkers, not talkers, not sleepers, not slaggers, not stragglers, etc., no, no, no. The future belongs to faster accurate runners. Runners are winners, and winners are runners. You must become faster and more accurate in your work.

> Know ye not that they which run in a race run all, but one receiveth the prize? So RUN, that ye may obtain. But I keep my body and bring it into subjection; lest that by any means, when I have preached to others, I myself should be a castaway. (1 Corinthians 9:24–27)

If you do not control your body, it will make you lose the prize awaiting you. Winning any race requires self-discipline. Restraining your mind to think right, and staying focused is mandatory for success in every aspect of your life and ministry.
Restrain your emotions.
Restrain your appetites.
Restrain your mouth—know when to speak and what to say.
Restrain your eyes to look ahead and stay focused on the prize.

God told Elijah "Go at once, I have commanded the widow in Zaraphath to care for you." Elijah did not see the widow nor eat the prepared cake, until he left where he was at once; in obedience to God's voice. (2 Kings 17)

God told Abraham to go to Mont Moriah and sacrifice his promised son Isaac. With a sense of urgency, Abraham got up EARLY the next morning with his son Isaac and his servants and began his journey in search of Mount Moriah. Abraham did not see the prepared lamb caught in the ticket for the sacrifice, until he left early from where he was, and arrived at the place God to him to go. (Genesis 22)

You will always discover God's supernatural provision, when you arrived on time at the place God tells you to go.

God's provisions are only for those who meet God's conditions. Both Abraham and Elijah were able to access God's provisions because they met God's conditions by their total obedience.

The Master gave the first servant five talents. He went at once and put his talent to work. His talents multiplied double because he put it to work at once. When the Master retuned to check on His gifts he invested in His servants, the first servant was given more rewards. He was honored and called a good and faithful servant, because he was very productive. He didn't sit on his gifts. He put them to work with a sense of urgency. The last servant was dishonored. He was called worthless and good for nothing. His gift was taken away from him because he was lazy and nonproductive. He buried his gift instead of putting it to work. Your Gifts or talents are not to be buried. They are to be developed, exposed and made marketable. (Matthew 25:15–30)

Timely right action is the difference between success and failure and sometimes even between life and death. Even the right decision made too late is of no effect.

- Some people die, not for the lack of medicine. They die for the lack of timely attention.
- Timing is everything.
- Timing determines the value of a thing and the impact of its results to the user.
- Everyone and everything is for a time and a reason.

The only time you have is *now*. Put the talent, gift, or skill to work now that God has given you and make the most of it. Every moment is your *now moment*.

If a person or thing cannot fulfill their reason for existence in their time, they become irrelevant, useless, unfulfilled, and miserable. Don't let the reason for your existence be unfulfilled while your time swiftly passes you by. Wake up and go to work. Now is your time.

Nothing is evaluated, validated, or appreciated based upon its pleasure but based upon the fulfillment of its purpose. Life is about purpose, not pleasure. You will never discover your purpose until you come to your creator-God. The purpose of a product is determined before it is made. A product does not give value to its purpose, but the purpose gives value to the product. Your true value in this world depends on your fulfillment of your God-given purpose. "Before you entered your mother womb, I knew you" (Jeremiah 1:5).

Sometimes, we spent all our lives chasing material things, comfort, and pleasure. Nothing is wrong with having good things if you get them honestly, but don't let the things have control over you. You will never find your purpose in things, but you can always accumulate things as you fulfill your purpose in life.

Time is the most valuable thing in this world. What good is a lot of money if you have no time to spend it? What good are material things if you have no time to enjoy it and no one to enjoy them with? Seek God for wisdom and understanding. They are necessities for successful living.

> Teach us to number our days so that we may apply hearts to wisdom. (Psalm 90:12)

> And I will say to my soul, Soul, thou hast much goods laid up for many years; take life easy, eat, drink and be merry. But God said unto him, You fool, *this very night*, you life will be demanded from you. Then who will get what you have prepared for yourself. (Luke 12:19)

There is no time without life, and there is no life without time. Your accomplishments and failures are determined by where you invest your time and efforts. Again, no matter who you are, where you are from, where you are located, or what your status in life is, everyone has equal amount of time every day. The presidents of nations, and the beggars at the street corner have the same twenty-four hours every day. Where you invest your time and efforts is where you will see the most results. Change your condition and create a better future by changing where you invest your time and efforts. Only a moment of life and time have been assigned to each one by God to fulfill his purpose on the earth.

> All people are like grass, and all the glory is like the flowers of the field. The grass withers and the flowers fall. (1 Peter 1:24)
>
> Why, you do not even know what will happen tomorrow. What is your life? You are a mist that appears for a little while and then vanishes. (James 4:14)

LIFE IS NOT AS LONG AS IT LOOKS. Life is so brief. Divert or invest your time, energy, and resources in the right things, right people, right jobs and right places. Your returns will be beneficial and rewarding. Only what we do for Christ is eternal. Everything you have is measured and limited. Be mindful of who and what you invest it in.

YOUR LIFE IS LIKE A FLASHING VAPOR. EVERYTHING AND EVERYONE THAT EXIST HAS AN EXPIRATION DATE. DON'T WASTE YOUR MOMENT. Learn to plan your days, weeks, and years in advance. It will enable you to make the most of your time, achieve your goals, and become the best you. Planning is aiming and aiming is planning. If you aim at nothing, you are guaranteed to miss everything. Be wise, stay focused and hurry up, because you do not know your expiration date. You have little time and a lot of greater things God wants to accomplish in and through you. Sober up, redeem the time, for the days are evil and short.

Now is the only time you have. The next minute could be your last minute. Get back up now. Run faster now. Get it done now. Humble yourself now. Forgive others and make up now. Make time for your family now. Procrastination kills purpose because everything is for a time and a reason. Procrastination will cause you to live an unfulfilled life. Procrastination will keep you struggling, and determination will keep you winning. Solution is in timely action.

Chapter 6

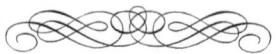

Stop Being Late
Latecomers Always Get Leftovers

Doing things early automatically puts you ahead in the game of life, and gives you advantages over your competitors. Doing things early delivers you from last-minute stress, poor performance, and unnecessary mistakes. Early the next morning, Abraham got up and returned to the place where he stood before the LORD. "How late are you for your prayer time or devotional time with God?" (Genesis 19:27).

How late are you for appointments with man? How late are you for work every week? Rising up early is a godly requirement for great accomplishments.

> Early the next morning Abraham got up and loaded his donkey. He took with him two of his servants and his son Isaac. When they had cut enough wood for the burnt offering, he set out for the place God had told him about. (Genesis 22:3)
>
> Early in the morning Joshua and all the Israelites set out from Shittim and went to

the Jordan, where they camp before crossing over. (Joshua 3:1)

O God, thou art my God; early will I seek thee: my soul thirsted for thee, my flesh longeth for thee in a dry and thirsty land, where no water is. (Psalm 63:1)

And in the morning, rising up a great while before day, He went out, and departed into a solitary place, and there prayed. (Mark 1:35)

Lateness prevents the fulfillment of purpose and causes you to pay more for less. If you were to order dinner for your guests, and the food arrived two hours late after your guest left, what good is the food?

Lateness restrains your potentials.

Lateness makes others question your ability to handle leadership responsibilities.

Lateness takes away from your personalities.

Lateness denies you entry.

Lateness is a prime thief of your resources. Every time you are late paying a bill, they charge you more.

Stop being late for everything. The more late you are in doing a thing, the less valuable it becomes and the lesser impact it has. Late comers are always embarrassed.

Pray for ideas, focus, think, be creative, do research, tap into all available resources, be humble, listen, take good advice, etc. Bottom line is, find a legal way to get it done because you are running out of time and time is running out.

Every day that goes by is one day deducted from all of our lives. You don't have time to fool around. There will be no perfect time. If it is not raining, it's going to be snowing. If it is not snowing, the sun will be shining very hot.

You are getting older, and your energy is measured. There will come a time, you will not be able to do what you can do now. That is why you need to rise up and do it now. "Arise, shine, for thy light is come, and the glory of the Lord is risen upon thee" (Isaiah 60:1).

Your shining is hidden in your rising. If you don't rise up, you will never shine. Your gift will make room for you if you develop it.

- The soundness of your mind is the power of great actions, and the constant use of your imagination is the creation of the unseen.

- When you look in God's direction, you will see your blessings flowing. When you stay in God's direction, you will keep your blessings flowing.

- In God's direction, you will find His provision and protection.

- We are the sum total of our thoughts and the multiplication of our actions.

- If the devil can gain control of your mind, he is in control of everything you say and do.

- If the word of God can control your mind, God is in control of everything you say and do.

- Look ahead and keep driving forward.

- Don't just be anybody; be the best body.

- Change is your opportunity to make your tomorrow better than your today.

Chapter 7

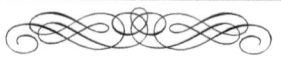

Stop Giving Excuses
The More Excuses You Give Yourself, The Less You Become Your Best

The more excuses you give yourself, the less you become your best. (Wow!) Excuses do not make your life better; they make your life stagnant. Excuses do not bring back the blessings you missed, because you could not do what was required, when it was required, and how it was required. One of the major enemies to your next level of success is convenience.

"See that no one is sexually immoral, or is godless like Esau, who for a single meal sold his inheritance rights as the oldest son. Afterward, as you know, when he wanted to inherit this blessing, he was rejected. Even though he sought the blessing with tears, he could not change what he had done" (Hebrews 12:16–17).

There are more good reasons why you need to rise up and become consistently committed, than there are reasons why you cannot do it.

Don't let your condition become your justification, for not getting to your divine destination. Four men had leprosy, but they did not allow their condition to prevent them from pressing forward to save their lives, and accomplish something great for their future.

"And there were four leprous men at the entering in of the gate: and they said one to another, why sit we here until we die?" (1 Kings 7:3).

The continuation of your life is in your future. Your life is at stake if you do nothing for your future, and your future is at stake if you do nothing with your life. Lord, help us. Life goes by faster than we planned and expect. We must learn to cease every precious moment and make the best of it because we might not have another one.

Don't waste your time on foolishness. God can do something for you and through you, that he has done for no one else. Believe and step out on faith. Only those who dare to try smarter and harder again, can break the borders of limitations placed on their lives.

Work

The better you want your life to become, the more responsibilities you have to accept, and the more initiatives you have to take. You are responsible for the results you desire; no one else is. Every help you receive is a favor, so be grateful and appreciate it.

Being responsible means making wise decisions and doing what needs to be done, with whom it needs to be done with, when it needs to be done, how it needs to be done, where it needs to be done, without being repeatedly told to do it.

Good results are never produced being complacent, they are produced by doing the right things at the right time. Work develops your gifts and skills. Work exposes the ideas, dreams, gifts, and skills you have hidden on the inside. Work brings you economic and social freedom and success. Your gift is a solution to somebody else's problem. You are paid for the problem you solve; on the other hand, you pay for the problem you create. Better to be paid than to pay. Good work puts you in demand and makes your gifts and skills marketable. Work is a stage to display your ideas, gifts, talents, and skills to the outside world. Work will make your dreams, visions, and goals become a reality.

It takes your personal, passionate, intentional, extraordinary work to produce extraordinary results. Work is required to make or build anything great. Work enhances creativity and enables good workers to discover the unknown. Work is an opportunity to make the invisible visible. That is why faith without works is dead.

> Even so faith, if it hath not works, is dead, being alone. Yea, a man say, Thou hast faith, and I have works: shew me thy faith without thy works, and I will shew thee my faith by my works. (James 2:17–18)

Workers are builders and builders are workers. If you will build any aspect of your life, consistent work is required by you. God worked six days to create the earth. If God could work, how about you? Anything that is not working is gotten rid of. Anything or anyone who is not doing what they were made to do, loses their relevance. "On the seventh day God ended His work which He had made; and He rested on the seventh day from all His WORK which He had made" (Genesis 2:2).

Go to work early. Work smarter, work harder, work faster, and maintain a positive attitude. You will succeed. Don't let your job affect you negatively; instead, you affect your job positively. Be a thermostat and not a thermometer. A thermostat sets the temperature for the surrounding atmosphere; whereas, a thermometer only records the temperature.

Your appearance, your facial expression, your choice of words, your tone of voice, your reaction to situation, and your approach to others all help to create a peaceful and productive work atmosphere.

- The more excuses you give yourself, the less you become your best. (Wow!)

- Excuses do not make your life better; they make your life stagnant.

- Excuses do not bring back the blessings you missed because you could not do what was required, when it was required, and how it was required.

- The continuation of your life is in your future.

- Your life is at stake if you do nothing for your future, and your future is at stake, if you do nothing with your life. (Lord, help us).

Chapter 8

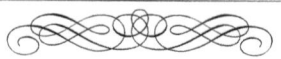

Trust

Trust is the greatest award anyone can achieve. Stuff is a byproduct of trust.

"Trust in the Lord with all thine heart; and lean not unto thine own understanding. In all thy ways acknowledge him, and he shall direct thy paths" (Proverbs 3:5–6).

Trust opens unending doors. Trust gives you access to the wealth of others. Trust puts you in charge when you ought not to be in charge. Trust causes people to be at ease around you. Trust makes your word valuable to others. Trust will cause you to be highly recommended. Trust will attract unending customers to the service you provide.

Trust is not earned by what you say repeatedly but what you do consistently. "They that trust in the Lord shall be as mount Zion, which cannot be removed, but abideth for ever" (Psalm 125:1).

Ask the Holy Spirit to help you build a good character. Adopt good habits and grow into a trustworthy lifestyle. It is necessary to live a peaceful and successful life. Anything dirty is always rejected. Dirty hands always leave behind retraceable print. Dirty deeds only stay cover for a short time.

Every best friend has a best friend that you don't know. What you think is a secret is already exposed to the world; it's just a matter of time. The things done in darkness come to light sooner than later. Anything you will be ashamed of publicly, try not do them in the dark, especially if it is something that will ruin your character.

When God or someone trusts you with their stuff, you are expected and required to do things their way, not yours. The easier way to lose access to many blessings is to keep betraying the trust placed in you and keep giving excuses for not doing what is expected. Trust demands being honest and treating others fairly whether you like them or know them. Never forget that the seeds you sow only bear fruits in your life.

Everything about God is based upon one word. That word is *trust*. Your level of trust in God, determines what you will receive from Him. God's level of trust in you, based upon your *faithfulness* with little in public and private, determines what God will continue to release to you. Can God trust you to do things His way? (Matthew 25:14–30).

When you want something from God, you must stay focused. Avoid distractions and fleshly gratification as much as possible. They are your two major enemies that will mislead to your disqualification. Distractions and fleshly gratification equal disqualification.

Never base your belief in God upon what makes sense or what you see with your natural eyes. God supersedes all of that. He is invisible and all-powerful. God can do anything, anywhere, and anytime. Your belief is your password to access your inheritance in Christ. "All things are possible to them that believe" (Mark 9:23). God never lack resources, even the things you cannot see with your natural eyes. Everything that you see with your eyes was made from what you don't see—that includes you and me. Once, we were not in existence physically, and now we are in existence. The invisible is the producer of the visible. God is a prepared God, and he deals with prepared people. You must become faster and more accurate in your work. When you want something made visible, look to God who is invisible, for His ideas because everything visible was once invisible.

By faith he left Egypt, not fearing the king's anger; he persevered because he saw him who is invisible. Hebrews 11:27

Colossians 3:16 (God of all visible and invisible)

The invisible is the producer of everything visible.

For by him were all things created, that are in heaven, and that are in earth, visible and invisible, whether they be thrones, or dominions, or principalities, or powers: all things were created by him, and for him: Colossians 1:16

Faith

Faith is the means by which you access what already exists for you in Christ Jesus. "Blessed be the God and Father of our Lord Jesus Christ, who hath blessed us with all spiritual blessings in heavenly places in Christ" (Ephesians 1:3). The purpose of faith is not get stuff from God but to develop trust in God.

Stuff is a byproduct of trust. God and man will give you stuff once you can prove yourself trustworthy. Faith comes by hearing Jesus, who is the living Word of God. Results come by obeying Jesus, who is the fulfilled Word of God. The place of trust is the place of faith. The place of faith is the place of God's pleasure. The place of God's pleasure is the place of God's power. The place of God's power is the place of unlimited miracles.

"But without faith it is impossible to please him: for he that cometh to God must believe that he is, and that he is a rewarder of them that diligently seek him" (Hebrews 11:6). Pleasing God instead of self is most important. In most cases, self cannot help self when it comes to real serious matters, but God can always help.

Everything about God is already done. Everything you will ever believe God for already exist. It's just the matter of you discovering it in the invisible realm, and releasing faith in God; for its materialization in the physical ream.

Faith requires faithfulness with what God has trusted you with, for there to be a continuous increase. You cannot be fruitful God's way, if you are not faithful. Prayer is like an express lane, and faith is like a U-Haul truck that gets your stuff from the invisible realm to the visible realm.

- Trust is the greatest award anyone can achieve.

- Stuff is a byproduct of trust.

- Trust is not earned by what you say repeatedly, but what you do consistently.

- When you want something from God, you must stay focused. Avoid distractions and fleshly gratification as much as possible. They are your two major enemies that will mislead to your disqualification.

- Distractions and fleshly gratification will lead to your disqualification from God's pending blessings for you.

- When you do not listen to God's warning privately, you will embarrass yourself publicly.

Chapter 9

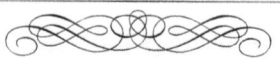

Consistent Prayer Life

There is no exchange for a consistent prayer life. I believe with all my heart that this is the most important chapter in this book. Developing a consistent prayer life is the key to experiencing what heaven can do on earth through you, for you, with you, and for others according to God plan and purpose.

- ➢ Prayer is the place of recognizing and understanding your needs, weakness, and inabilities.
- ➢ It is the place of recognizing how badly you need God because without him you are nothing.
- ➢ Prayer is the place of acknowledging God's absolute sovereignty over everything that is and is to come.
- ➢ Prayer is the place of tapping into God's mighty power to deliver, provide, and protect by faith.
- ➢ Prayer is a place of divine insight and revealed truth.
- ➢ Prayer is the place of shifting your belief from your inabilities to God's infinite abilities to do everything and anything at the same time all the times.
- ➢ Prayer is the most unrestricted all-purpose, powerful tool any believer can use.
- ➢ Prayers cause heaven to do the impossible on earth for you, with you and through you.
- ➢ Prayer attracts divine favor from God and with man.

- Prayer is the place where heaven deposits and earth receives.
- Prayer is talking less to man and listening more to God.
- Prayer is like oxygen for your spirit as a believer.
- Prayer is the only place where a believer can exhale problems and breathe in solutions.
- Your prayers are the legs that keep things moving in your favor.
- When you stop praying, things stop moving in your favor.
- Prayer is your situational control center.
- Prayer is the place of exercising the power of Jesus over Satan and the forces of darkness.
- Consistent prayers make all the difference. Go back to prayer.
- "Prayer is a place of many great rewards" (Matthew 6:9).

The heaven is superior to the earth because the heaven was created first then the earth. "In the beginning God created the heaven and the earth" (Genesis 1:1). The heaven is position above the earth. Whatever is above is superior to that which is below. The heavens control the light system of the earth. If the heavens do not give light to the earth, the earth will be in total darkness (Genesis 1:14).

The heaves controls the seasons of the earth (Gen.1:14–15). When heavens release the sunshine, earth has a good day. When the heaven releases a storm, earth has a bad day. Technology and all the superpowers of the world combined cannot do anything about it.

Encounter with heaven brings a permanent change. After their personal encounters with God, Jacob was changed from being a cunning man to the nation of Israel. His sons formed the twelve tribes of Israel. Saul was noted for murdering Christians but he was transformed into the Apostle Paul. The

Apostle Paul wrote two thirds of the Bible. If you want your season to change on earth to fulfill God's purpose and if you want your season to change from nothing to everything, you must patiently look to the heavens and begin to walk in total obedience to God's Word. Ask the Holy Spirit to help you. You must learn to obey God regardless of situation or circumstance. Your blessing is wrapped up in your obedience to God. Your obedience is God's wall of protection around you, and your household from the enemy, his agents, and devices. Your obedience is also God's direction for invisible provision to you from His designated supplier.

You don't even know what means God is going to use to supply your needs and wants. All you have to do is obey His voice and His Word whether it makes sense or not. Most times, God's designated supplier is in disguise; that's why your eyes must stay on Him and your ears must remain attentive to His voice.

When you walk in disobedience, you break down God's protective wall around you and your household and cause the enemy attacks to affect you and your household. When you consistently walk in obedience, the enemy's attacks do not accomplish its ordained results; but when you disobey, it does. Your disobedience is the security pass you give to the enemy to access your territory to steal, kill, and destroy.

God is like the richest businessman who releases continuous blessings and rewards to those who willingly release their faith. They release their faith to enter a covenant of obedience with him. He is our heavenly Father who loves and cares for his children unconditionally. Everything about God is a trade. Mistakenly, we trade the enormous blessing from heaven for temporary fleshly gratifications. Stop trading blessing. Blessing sustains, protects, and provides; whereas, fleshly behavior always leads to spiritual death. Blessings and benefits come with position.

Your level of position determines your level of authority, the magnitude of your words, and amount of benefits you receive. It is because of our position in Christ, we are seated far above principalities and powers (Ephesians 1:20, 2:6).

We are daily loaded with benefits. Without position, there are no benefits and authority. When God positions you, you are responsible to protect your position by your total obedience to God.

Pay attention!

Position comes with accountability and blessings. Blessings come with responsibilities. Responsibility is doing what needs to be done, when it needs to be done, how it needs to be done without being repeatedly told to do it. Your next blessing depends on your current blessings. Be faithful with what you have now; it controls what you will receive next. Protect your position in Christ at all cost, or else your end will be pitiful.

When Adam disobeyed, he lost his position with his benefits and authority. His disobedience affected the entire human race.

When you consistently disobey God without repentance, it does not just only affect you. It affects everything connected to you.

Some Hindrances to Answers to Prayers

1. *Doubt*. Doubt is a thief of your prepaid blessings. "But when you ask, you must believe and not doubt, because the one who doubts is like the wave of the sea, blown and tossed by the wind. That person should not expect to receive anything from the Lord, Such a double-mind and unstable in all they do" (James 1:6–8). Then Jesus told him, "Because you have seen me, you have believed; blessed are those who have not seen and yet have believed" (John 20:29)

2. *Impatience*. Anxiousness always causes people to miss out on the best answers to their prayers. Blessings

delayed are never blessings denied. All trees don't bear fruit at the same time. God will do for you what He has not done for anyone if you ask Him, believe Him, and be led by His Spirit daily. The LORD always saves the *best* for those who wait for Him. "Jesus turned Water into the best wine at the very last minute, when there was no wine" (John 2).

Wait especially when you don't have peace in your heart about what you are about to do. Wait, don't do things because others are doing it and it looks like it is working. Wait, God is at work on your behalf behind the scene. Wait, God will come through for you in style when and how you least expect. *Wait.*

> Do not be anxious about anything, but in every situation, by prayer and petition, with thanksgiving present your request to GOD. (Philippians 4:6)

> But they that wait upon the LORD shall renew their strength, they shall mount up with wings as eagles; they shall run and not be weary; and they shall walk and not faint. (Isaiah 40:31)

> Abraham asked, believed, and waited for God; God came through with Isaac the promised son (Genesis 21:12). Hannah asked, believed, and waited for God; God came through with Samuel, the greatest prophet in Israel (1 Samuel 1). Zacharias and Elizabeth prayed and waited upon God; God came through with John the Baptist (Luke 1).

Personal testimony: Four years after we got married, my wife and I had no children. She visited several hospitals and prominent doctors and underwent several tests. X-rays showed that her womb was filled with fibers.

The doctors diagnosed that her chances of having biological children was 0 percent, but God, who is rich in mercies, proved the doctors and technology wrong. June of 2017, our oldest graduated from one of the best high schools in the USA. She was an honor student with excellent character from elementary through high school.

3. *Not asking precisely for what you need or want.* "If you ask anything in my name, I will do it" (John 14:14). "Ask, and it shall be given you; seek, and ye shall find; knock, and it shall be opened unto you: For every one that asketh receiveth; and he that seeketh findeth; and to him that knocketh it shall be opened" (Matthew 7:7–8).

4. *Habitual sin and intentional disobedience.* This is when you make sin a habit because you know forgiveness and restoration are available through the shared blood of Jesus when you repent. Sometimes our greatest blessings are not in our combined human efforts and connection but in our simple instant obedience to God. It pays to obey God.

As a believer, you must understand that sin is not a kite or parachute that keeps you flying high; instead, it is a heavy weight that weighs you down from grace to disgrace. No matter what form sin takes, whether attractive, lucrative, momentary, pleasurable, etc., sin will always bring people down at the end.

Sin always kicks people out of their position of spiritual and physical authority. The scripture reveals that sin kicked Adam and Eve out of their blessed position in the Garden of Eden. Sin kicked Sampson out his position as a judge in Israel.

It's best to ask God for forgiveness and those you offend when you sin, rather than to pretend or keep trying to cover your tracks of wrongdoings. Jesus paid the full price for all of our sins so that the Holy Spirit can help us modify the deeds of our body. As we grow in the LORD, we ought to progressively become like Him in our image and likeness instead of being like the devil in our thoughts and behavior.

"Righteousness exalts a nation; but sin is a reproach to any people" (Proverbs 14:34). The Holy Spirit helps everyone who desires to grow above the habit of sin by daily renewing their minds with the Word of God, spending time in consistent prayers and Christ-like fellowship.

> What shall we say then? Shall we continue in sin, that Grace may abound? (Romans 6:1–2)

> Wherefore seeing we also are compassed about with so great a cloud of witnesses, let us lay aside every weight, and the sin which doth so easily beset us, and let us run with patience the race that is set before us. (Hebrews 12:1)

God forbid. How shall we that are dead to sin live any longer therein? Remember, there are no secrets on earth. Everything will be discovered sooner or later. It has been proven over and over again: the same person you commit a crime with is the same person whose mind is influenced to turn you in. As seen on the media, all sex scandals are reported by those who were once sex partners.

Unforgiveness. "If I regard iniquity in my heart, the LORD will not hear me" (Psalm 66:16).

"And when you stand praying, forgive, if ye have ought against any; that your Father also which is in heaven may forgive you your trespasses" (Mark 11:35).

Take a Stand in Prayer

Impossible favorable results are for those who take an immovable stand in the Spirit.

> Wherefore take unto you the whole armour of God, that ye may be able to withstand in the evil day, and having done all to stand. Stand therefore, having your loins girt about with truth, and having on the breastplate of righteousness; a stand is a non-retreating, ever advancing position rooted in the power of God. (Ephesians 6:13–14)

The Holy Spirit is the place of all supplies, and the flesh is the place of all needs. The devil is a wicked spirit. He is not care giver, and he is never deterred by your politeness or ignorance of his agenda to steal, kill, and destroy.

"From the days of John the Baptist until now the kingdom of Heaven suffereth violence, and the violent take it by force" (Matthew 11:12).

You must always deal with the devil consistently with maximum spiritual force:

- Applying the superior blood of Jesus against his works and agents.
- Meditating, believing, and declaring the Word of God
- Functioning under the anointing of the Holy Spirit
- Casting out demonic spirits
- Binding the powers of darkness and loosing the blessings of God
- Calling those things which are not as though they were all in the name of Jesus.

Here are a few biblical heroes who took a stand in prayer and fasting and enforced the victory of the cross by faith:

1. Jacob: He took an immovable stand in the Spirit, and after his encounter with heaven, his name was changed to Israel, which became a nation. "I will not let you go until you bless me" (read Genesis 32:24–29).
2. David: He took an immovable stand in the Spirit. "Who is this uncircumcised Philistine, that he should defy the armies of the living God?" (Read 1 Samuel 17:26–36.)
3. Hannah: She took an immovable stand in the Spirit. After being barren all her life, she conceived and gave birth to the greatest prophet in Israel, Samuel. In addition, God blessed her with five more children. (Read 1 Samuel 1 and 1 Samuel 2:21).
4. Hezekiah: He took an immovable stand in the Spirit. After receiving his death news, he turned his face to the wall in prayer, and God heard him and added fifteen more years to his life. (Read 2 Kings 20:2–6).
5. Esther: She took an immovable stand in the Spirit, and all the plot and the enemies of the Jews were destroyed. "If I perish, I perish" (read Esther 4:16).

Thank God for medical science, technology, good doctors and engineers, education, high political positions, fame, massive wealth and riches, etc. All those things are good, but our faith does not rest in any of those things. They are all subject to failure one way or the other. Our faith is never in the wisdom of man; it is rooted in the power of God. Read 1 Corinthians 2:4–5.

You must learn to resist and oppose the works of darkness by faith, or else they will remain tormenting you (James 4:7, 1 Peter 5:9).

The Spirit Realm Is a Place of All Supplies

Position yourself to receive from God by your obedience. Maintain your position by your character. Advance your position by your sacrificial service to the Lord. Every blessing has a maintenance plan. Your consistent obedience and maintaining a godly character in public and private, are the maintenance requirements for every blessing you receive.

The heaven is the seat, the royal throne of God. It is God's office and the place of final decisions, all authority, all powers, all possibilities, and the place that lacks no supplies. It is also God's home, God's dwelling place. A place of beauty beyond descriptions and Precisions. A place of joy, unspeakable glory, and splendor. A place of eternal life and peace that passes all understanding. Oh, the beauty, splendor, and powers or heaven in the dwelling place of God.

Only Earthly Needs Bring Heavenly Visits

There must be a need on earth for there to be a visit from heaven. If there are no demands from earth, there will be no supply from heaven. The heavens are always overstocked with resources, and the earth is always depleted of resources.

Jesus only visited those who were in need, so if you have a need, release your faith and expect a visit. In fact, it was the need for mankind's redemption from death (eternal separation from God) and hell (place for those who reject Christ); that brought Christ into the world.

Needs backed by expectation of God's fulfillment lead to miracles (supernatural happenings). God reveals himself to His own as He chooses. Through that revelation, believer gets to know something or some attributes about God. Their knowledge of who God is, enable them to trust and love Him more. Those who do not believe in Jesus Christ, do not deserve such precious revelation that produces knowledge about God.

God's children are entitled to that knowledge, because that knowledge increases their faith in God. Faith in God moves obstacles out of the way.

God requires order, dedication, and sacrifice, which lead to promotion and increase. Beauty is always seen in its fullest when things and people are in order.

Divine Signals

Divine signals are pointers to major breakthroughs and preventers of major problems, so be led by the Spirit. "For as many as are led by the Spirit of God, are the children of God" (Romans 8:14). Being led by God's Spirit is proof that you are a child of God. Anything the Spirit of God leads you to do will be backed by the Word of God, the protection of God, and the provisions of God. The Holy Spirit will speak to your spirit in time and on time, so you can act on His Word and harvest the blessings.

Understanding the season you are in and Spirit-led timely actions can produce a miraculous harvest. God makes all things beautiful in His time, not yours. When you are not led by God's Spirit, you can easily be deceived by the devil.

"And no marvel; for satan himself is transformed into an angel of light" (2 Corinthians 11:14).

Only the Holy Spirit knows your blessings' manifestation timing. Eyes have not seen nor ears heard what God has in store for those who love Him, but it has been revealed by His Spirit. "The Holy Spirit is all powerful, he can do all things" (1 Corinthians 2:9–15).

"Then he answered and spake unto me, saying, This is the word of the LORD unto Zerubbabel, saying, NOT by might, nor by power, but by my spirit, saith the LORD of hosts" (Zechariah 4:6).

The Holy Spirit can only work where the Word of God has been received and believed.

- Prayer is the place of shifting your belief from your inabilities to God's infinite abilities to do everything and anything at the same time, all the time.

- Prayer is the most unrestricted all-purpose, powerful tool any believer can use.

- Prayers cause heaven to do the impossible on earth for you, with you and through you.

- Prayer attracts divine favor from God and with man.

- Prayer is the place where heaven deposits, and earth receives.

- Prayer is talking less to man and listening more to God.

- Only earthly needs bring heavenly visits.

- Divine signals are pointers to major breakthroughs and preventers of major problems, so be sensitive to the leading the Holy Spirit.

CHAPTER 10

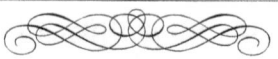

Life is Sustained by Good Relationships and Smart Work

Relationship is the mother of all lives. Everything living and nonliving is birthed out of relationships. Our main purposes of existence as human beings for the limited time we have on earth are as follows:

(a) To develop a personal relationship with God by receiving His only begotten Son, Jesus Christ, as our personal LORD and Savior.
(b) To maintain an active personal with God by the help and guidance of the Holy Spirit. Daily and intentionally, you have to meditate on God's Word, spend quality time in prayers, and become actively involved in a Bible-based, Spirit-filled, Christ-centered church.
(c) To advance our relationship with God, by our total obedience to God's Word and voice. We must daily yield to the guidance of the Holy Spirit in order to fulfill God's purpose in and through us.
(d) Initiate, develop, and maintain good relationship with our fellowman.

Maintaining a personal relationship with God through His son, Jesus Christ, determines where and how your soul will spend eternity. Maintaining good relationship with your fellowman, especially good people, will determine the level of support you will receive in every aspect of your life here on earth.

Invest your time, services, and resources in maintaining good relationships. Call your good friends and check on them at least once a week and visit them at least twice a month.

No one fully fulfills his purpose here on earth successfully without initiating, maintaining, and advancing good relationship with others. You are responsible to initiate, maintain, and advance your relationship with people are godly, kind, wise, experienced, legal, and effective people. Find them and invest in quality relationship with them. Your returns will surpass your investment by wide margins. The input from these people in your life makes a big positive difference. Not everyone godly has mature in demonstrating kindness to others. Not everyone kind has a personal relationship with God through Jesus Christ. Not everyone godly and kind is effective in other matters of life that are needed. Not everyone effective is wise. There is a need to develop good relationship with godly people for godly wisdom, intercession on your behalf, spiritual nurturing, and guidance in the things of God. There is a need for wise and experienced people. They provide knowledge and guidance in the right path, to save you from wasting time and making bad choices. There is a need for effective people to get things done in a timely and excellent manner. There is a need for kind people to give you timely resources needed to fulfill goals and visions and to deliver you from the bondage of all forms of lack or debt.

Kindness is a bridge that crosses someone over a river of need(s) they could have drowned in. Good relationship with the right people always pays off well in unexpected, timely, needed manners. Good relationship with the right people is priceless. Relationships are like banks. What you put in grows with time, multiplies and comes back to you in various forms; at different times and season.

It is the right thing to reach out to everyone with the love of God and a helping hand, but it is necessary and wise to prayerfully choose those you allow in your inner circle or partner with.

Jesus Christ, who is our example, prayed all night for divine wisdom and direction before choosing twelve out of many men with various character and career as His disciple and friends.

"And it came to pass in those days, that he went out unto a mountain to pray, and continued all night in prayer to God. And when it was day, he called unto him his disciples and chose twelve whom also he named apostles" (Luke 6:12–13).

If Jesus, who is God, could pray all night before choosing His apostles and friends, how about you? Be very mindful of who you make your friend. Those you surround yourself with will influence your mind-set, decisions, and actions. They will push you up or bring you down. They will be a blessing or a destruction to your future. Your association and conversations will impact your destiny in a positive or negative way. "Be not deceived: evil communication corrupt good manners" (1 Corinthians 15:33).

Again, I say, not everyone you like, needed in your close circle. Not everyone you like, you can trust for your well-being. Not everyone who claims they like you, honestly likes you. You are only a tool for their convenience, pleasure, and comfort. Not everyone with you is for you. For example, Judas Iscariot, one of Jesus's own disciples betrayed him for thirty pieces of silver.

"And Judas Iscariot one of the twelve, went unto the chief priests, to betray him unto them" (Mark 14:10). Delilah pretended like she loved Samson. She seduced and deceived him. She was intimate with Samson, and he told her the secret of his strength. She betrayed him to his enemies.

"And when Delilah saw that he had told her all his heart, she sent and called for the lords of the Philistines, saying, come up this once, for he hath shewed me all his heart. Then the lords of the Philistines came up unto her, and brought money in hand" (Judges 16:18). Joseph brothers envied him and out of jealousy sold him for twenty pieces of silver (Genesis 37:28).

Then there passed by Midianites merchantmen, and they drew and lifted up Joseph out of the pit and sold Joseph to the Ishmeelites for twenty pieces of silver. They brought Joseph to Egypt. It takes a consistent prayer life to discern the spirit of a person. Looks are deceiving in most cases. Even the devil knows how to make up, dress up, and look flashy.

"And no marvel; for Satan himself is transformed into an angel of light" (2 Corinthians 11:14).

The human body is the house and carrier of the person's spirit and soul. Man is a speaking spirit with a soul and lives in a body. Every human body contains a spirit. After receiving Christ, a believer receives a new spirit by faith. Bottom line is, spirits cannot be seen with the natural eyes. You cannot tell that a man, woman, boy, or girl is blessed or cursed just by looking at their outward appearance, or material possessions with your natural eyes.

A good-looking person with a lot of material possession can be cursed, because of their consistent disobedience to God. A not-so-good-looking person can be so blessed and peaceful, because of their consistent obedience to God and vice versa.

"A new heart also will I give you, and a new spirit will I put within you; and I will take away the stony heart out of your flesh, and I will give you an heart of flesh" (Ezekiel 36:26). Every human body contains a spirit and soul that is blessed because of their consistent obedience to God or cursed because of their consistent disobedience to God.

> And all these blessings shall come on thee, and overtake thee, if thou shalt hear-

> ken unto the voice of the Lord thy God. (Deuteronomy 28:2)
>
> But it shall come to pass, if thou wilt not hearken unto the voice of the Lord thy God, to observe to do all his commandments and his statues which I command thee this day; that all these curses shall come upon thee, and overtake thee. (Deuteronomy 28:15)

Sometimes letting the wrong people in the inner circle of your life because of looks, sweet talk, flashy things, and money can cost your very life in the end. Be prayerful about close relationships. Be willing to let go and disconnect when it is not right, especially if you all are not married God's way.

The story is told of Jonah trying to flee from his assignment from God. He was under the curse of disobedience. He boarded a ship heading to Tarshish. God sent a great storm on the sea, because of Jonah's disobedience. It almost caused the ship to wreck. The mariners and the ship captain were afraid, so they began to cast lots to find out the cost of the sudden evil to come upon them. The lot fell on Jonah. Bottom line is the moment they threw Jonah overboard, the storm ceased. Some folks are carriers and distributors of trouble and confusion. As long as they are in your inner circle, there will be trouble and confusion. Let them go now so that peace and joy can come back to your life.

> But the Lord sent a great wind into the sea, and there was a mighty tempest in the sea, so that the ship was like to be broken. (Jonah 1:4)
>
> Any they said everyone to his fellow, Come, and let us cast lots, that we may know for

> whose cause this evil is upon us. So they cast lots, and the lot fell upon Jonah. (Jonah 1:7)

> So they took up Jonah, and cast him forth into the sea; and the sea ceased from her raging. (Jonah 1:15)

It is wise to connect with sound-headed people who are heading in your direction. It takes two wires of the same grade to be connected to a light switch and fixture for the light to come on. If the grades of the wires are different, the light never comes on. The only thing you will get is continuous short socket. If you connect with people who are not spiritually and mentally at your level, all you will get in return is headaches, confusion, and trouble as long as you all are together.

"Iron sharpeneth iron; so a man sharpeneth the countenance of his friend" (Proverbs 27:17). Wood can never sharpen iron, and water and fire don't mix. Life is too short to waste it with the wrong people. Some folks will not change. You will have to prayerfully make a change as God directs you.

If your friends do not have most of these character traits—God-fearing, honest, respectful, reliable, discipline, humble, helpful, peaceful, encouraging, truthful, upfront, take corrections and remain positive, challenge you to go forward to better your life, challenge you to maintain your integrity, and do the right things in public and private—you strongly need to consider choosing new friends.

Reaching out to people is a good thing, connecting with people is a better thing, but influencing people to move higher and forward in the right direction is the best thing.

You must reach out to others in order to connect with them, and you must connect with others in order to influence them. It is wise and also right to take the initiative to know and understand people instead of making conclusion about them based on assumptions. You can miss out on some of the greatest people on earth if you only reach out to those of your kind.

Again, we remind ourselves that man is a spirit with a soul living in a body. Our bodies are just the house for our spirit and soul. Some folks live in white house; others live in black, dark-brown, light-brown, tan, etc. Bottom line is we never see the real person on the inside because spirit and soul cannot be seen. We only hear them speak, and we feel or see their actions.

Constant clear communication is one of the keys to maintaining good relationship. Listen and understand what others are saying instead of always trying to express how right your view is. It is wise to settle issues as quickly as they arise in a relationship than to hold speech, stay angry, negative, and separate. Remember, when you separate from a friend from a friend, you are not just losing the bad characteristics of the person but the good ones too. It's always better to make up, and if you have to exit, exit peacefully. "A friend loveth at all times, and a brother is born for adversity" (Proverbs 17:17).

- It is wise to connect with sound-headed people who are heading in your direction.

- Constant clear communication is one of the keys to maintaining good relationship.

Conclusion

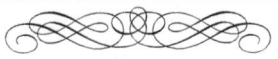

"Though thy beginning was small, yet thy latter end should greatly increase" (Job 8:7). God can work through you to make the best of all your leftovers. Put all your problems in God's hands. His hands are big enough to cover you from the storms of life. His hands are strong enough to fight all your enemies and win. His hands are soothing enough to ease your pain and heal your spirit, soul, and body. His hands are skillful enough to put your broken pieces back together and make your life whole and new again. His hands are powerful enough to remove obstacles out your way and guide you safely to your glorious destiny. Park your life in Jesus's body, soul, and spirit-made new shop. He will give you life and make you whole again if you let Him.

What matters most is not what you are dealing with but whose hands it's in. God only receives, blesses, breaks, multiplies, and gives back that which is given to him first.

The Bible narrates several examples:

> The Widow in Zarephath had her last flour and a little bit of oil left. She was about to make a small cake for she and her son to eat and die. The Prophet who was sent by God told her to make him a cake first. When she put what she had left in the hands of God through His servant, she was tremendously

> blessed. She never ran out of flour and oil. (1 Kings 17:9–16)

> The little boy had his lunch of five loaves of bread and two fish in the midst of five thousand hungry men, not counting women and children. He willing gave his lunch to Jesus. Jesus received his lunch, blessed it, broke it and it multiplied as he give it back to the people. 5,000 men plus women and children were fed with more than enough including the boy who gave his lunch. (Matthew 14:17–21)

God is the potter, and we are clay vessels. He has the power and skills to remake us again into someone better and greater if we let him.

> But we have this treasure in jars of clay to show that this all-surpassing power is from God and not from us. (2 Corinthians 4:7)

> So I went down to the Porter house, and I saw him working at the wheel. 4 But the pot he was shaping from the clay was marred in his hands; so the Porter formed it into another pot, shaping it as seemed best to him. (Jeremiah 18:3)

About the Author

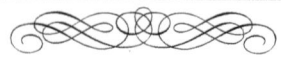

Pastor Kornah Flowers is a multigifted international motivational speaker. He is very passionate about prayer and youth development. He is the founder and senior pastor of Change Your Thinking International Church, Baltimore, Maryland. You can listen to many of Kornah Flowers inspiring sermons on Youtube. Pastor Flowers has earned his degree from National Bible College and Seminary. He is married and is father of three children, two biological and one adopted.